Silver-Coated Clay

by

Felicia Johnson

To Ellen,
You are my bestest
friend and I love
you dearly and
thank God for you!
You are a blessing!
Felicia
2/09

PublishAmerica
Baltimore

Dedication

I dedicate this book to my four wonderful children,
Joel, Matthew, Marie and Krystal,
who fill my life with joy, laughter and surprises and
to people like me who have struggled
against rejection and poor self-esteem.

Acknowledgments

I would like to thank my friend Debbie Davis, who long ago planted a seed of confidence when she said one day, "You should write a book."

This seed was watered by my in-laws, Walter Irvin Johnson II and the late Gloria L. Johnson. Dad Johnson, a former college professor, painstakingly edited and critiqued my work. The quoted words on the back cover text are his. Mom Johnson listened enthusiastically as her husband read the earliest version of my manuscript to her. My sister-in-law, Lorraine, took precious time to read through it and offered suggestions. Their interest and positive feedback watered the idea of bringing my book to publication.

I give many thanks to my husband, Walter Irvin Johnson III, who has played a vital role in the progress of not only my book, but of my life. I owe him first for being a hero and then for assisting me with this work by reading over numerous revisions, patiently listening to my thoughts, offering countless suggestions and keeping the children occupied while I was glued to the chair at my computer desk. His encouragement and support during the years of writing this book have been tireless and priceless. Irvin—I love you.

I would also like to thank the people who nourished my writing by sharing their memories: my mother, Aunt Mary, Aunt Lucille and Aunt Evelyn and every single person who has given me permission to print their names in my story.

I thank my mother, Marie Ward, for her tremendous sacrifice and love from the very beginning of my life and for her husband, Haywood Ward, who received my siblings and me with arms open wide.

I am deeply grateful for my pastors Joe and Lynn McKelvey, under whose dynamic ministry I continue to grow, and for my precious family in Christ at Christian Faith Fellowship Family Church.

Finally and forever, I thank the Lord. All the good in my life is because of Jesus.

Table of Contents

Chapter 1

News

"He shall not be afraid of evil tidings his heart is fixed, trusting in the Lord."
Psalm 112:7 (King James Version)

It was a Monday in January 2001. I stood at a place in time I thought I'd never reach. As a teenager, I figured my life in this world would end sometime around 1984. My expectation had something to do with a book written by George Orwell, the church people's talk of the Lord's soon return, and an intense desire to leave this old, evil world. At that time in my life, when I should have been having lots of fun, I often just wished I could die and go on up yonder to paradise. God had other plans. Now I stood at an important precipice in time. I felt small as I contemplated this momentous point in history; a point growing from the beginning of the work week, to the first month of the year, to the onset of another decade, to the turn of a century, to the dawn of a new millennium looming large before me.

I was grateful to have made it this far, but life wasn't getting any easier. First, we all had to deal with the weather which seemed to be getting more and more vicious. Winter pointed an icy forefinger in our direction as it made a grand and flashy entrance, knocking us New Yorkers over. It dumped several blizzards loaded with record amounts of snow upon us, which in turn overthrew schedules all over the tri-state area. Civic, religious, social and school events were cancelled. Stores, malls and professional offices were closed. Travel plans were crushed. Roads were blocked, highways shut down. Cities, towns and villages turned into states of emergency.

Secondly, certain body parts which I hardly noticed started talking, even complaining. I never heard much from my knees, esophagus and lower back until now. It was a bit eerie realizing that I was leaving my physically care-free youth behind. My husband Irvin, two years older than I, was the first to feel the effects of age creeping on, as he struggled with exhaustion, back pain, and aches in his knees and ankles. I'd chide him for acting old. Then I'd go through the same scenarios soon after him. During this decade, I would gain pounds that were impossible to lose without daily strenuous workouts for which I had no time, watch in horror as my facial and stomach muscles sagged southward and understand completely why people wore glasses that required the head to move up and down in order to focus near or far.

Thirdly, society itself was getting crazier. America's political system was rattled by a vicious fight at the polls. During the 2000 presidential election, Mr. George Bush won by just a hair and the opponent, Mr. Al Gore (incumbent Bill Clinton's vice-president), demanded a recount. Basic fundamentals such as marriage, family, and truth were being battled in the courtrooms. Too many children were growing up disturbed and neglected, leading some to commit horrible crimes of mass murder in school.

The financial world was unleashing its own set of headaches. Stocks plummeted. Fuel prices rose. Smaller companies were swallowed up by the giants, businesses collapsed, lawsuits increased and outsourcing work to cheap foreign labor got trendy. Though we avoided the big computer meltdown feared in 2000, the ability to find long-term employment in the corporate world, with paid health insurance and a great retirement package, became an endangered phenomenon. Times were definitely more perilous than ever.

To add to my stress, my husband was still a commuter. He was entering his fourteenth year of commuting to work sixty miles one way. Living in Orange County and isolated from relatives, I was alone each workday to handle the care of our three children, the house repairs, the front and back yard, the laundry, the meals, the shopping, the cleaning, the mail, the phone calls, the neighbors' requests, school issues, homework, doctor appointments, dental visits, etc. Instead of being the time of an exciting new millennium, the season was dismal. Life was feeling old at forty-one. It was as though I was on the verge of the winter of my life.

I thought that some good news from the extended family would have been very uplifting, especially after hearing all the bad news in the media. That was not about to happen.

My father had been sick and alone during the holiday. Neil, my brother and still a relatively young man at thirty-six, lived with Dad but I could not blame him if he needed a change of pace for the holidays. Shortly before Christmas Day, Neil hopped on a bus in Riverdale, Maryland, and six hours later relaxed in the cheery and festive home of our mother and stepfather in Mount Vernon, NY.

After the holiday, Neil returned home. News traveled slowly back from Riverdale. By the time I learned that Dad was in the hospital, he had been in intensive care for two weeks. I gathered from the sketchy account that Dad had gone to church on Christmas Eve and passed out. Four days later, on December 29, Neil helped to get him to a hospital in Baltimore.

As soon as I received the news from Mom, I called the hospital. After dialing several times and speaking to operators, I heard Dad on the line. He sounded very weak and his speech was slurred and garbled, which may have been the result of heavy medications.

"Eee-e-lo?" he exhaled.

"Hi, Dad…this is Felicia. How are you?"

"Oh…oh…I'm doing…okay. Uh…I wan you…to sell the house…and git me…a zenior…zit'zen's 'par'men," he panted out between breaths.

Wow, now he wants to move into a senior citizen's apartment, I thought. I had offered to help him sell his home a year ago when he was strong enough to assist me in the complex process of relocating.

"I'll look into it and see what I can do," I answered, but I already knew it was too late.

"I will be coming down to see you soon," I offered weakly.

"No, no…don' come; …wait till…I'm bedda."

A boxer's blow to the chest would not have deflated me more. I thought that Dad would be open to help now that he was in the hospital, desperately sick and flat on his back. I felt rejected and worthless. Aren't children supposed to be at their parent's side when it gets this bad? It was a painful reminder of the gulf between us.

A few days passed and I called again. This time I was able to get information from a nurse. She told me that Dad had fallen down when trying to rise from the hospital room chair.

Now I was worried. Fallen down?!?! Daddy never fell down. In my little girl mind, he was always big, tall and strong in body and in will. He towered over me in strength, knowledge and confidence. I was a puny, insignificant weakling next to him. Nobody ever stopped him or stood in his way. He did what he wanted and went where he desired. He was mighty, powerful and courageous. Why, he could eat sour cream from the container with a tablespoon and guzzle down a pint of buttermilk without gagging!

My dad—a tower of confidence and strength.(Korea, early 1950s)

I snapped back to the present. The image I had of him failed to hold ground in my adult world. Daddy had fallen down.

Glimpses of my dad as a very young and good-looking man.

After his remark, my desire to visit him was hindered by fear. I did not want to be subjected to belittlement, rejection or ridicule. If I went he probably would not even appreciate it. That would be too much to bear. Or he might treat me like a stranger, calling me any name that came into his head but the one Mom gave me. I could imagine him referring to me as "that skinny-legged woman over there" or limiting our communication to request for food and drink as though I was nothing more than a passing maid. Feelings of worthlessness might surface again and sap my strength. I needed to be strong now. I had a family.

I also had a part-time job as an office assistant, working three days a week to bring in extra money and three children who were in school. I did not want to throw our schedules out of whack when Dad didn't want me. I decided to visit when it was convenient, which was during the three-day weekend in honor of Dr. Martin Luther King's birthday.

When that time came however, I instead chose to take it easy and let our five-year-old daughter Marie attend her friend's birthday party. I thought it was a good plan since I needed some time to relax at home and I knew my husband needed time off the road after commuting all week.

We stayed home but I thought of Dad constantly. I was very concerned about him and continued calling the hospital every few days to check on his condition. It was a frustrating experience. I spoke mainly to receptionists and recordings since Dad was not able to answer the phone.

A nurse told me that they were planning on moving Dad out of intensive care and placing him into a regular room. I was filled with hope. If he is out of intensive care, there is a chance he will get better, mend his ways and rise up to finally bless his children.

On Monday evening, January 22, my mind was full of thoughts as I stood in a very used spot in my home—the narrow working kitchen. I wished we had a bigger kitchen. It didn't bother me when it was just Irvin and I or when the boys were little, but now we are a family of five and the boys were close to six feet tall. We did not fit very well in a space only thirty-six inches wide. Whenever someone decided to help me in the kitchen, instead of being grateful, I got annoyed that, at every turn, he was in my way. We just needed a larger home. I was thankful for my home, but we were really feeling crowded. The five of us were using up every inch of the middle-unit, three-bedroom, fourteen-hundred-square-foot townhouse, without a garage, attic or basement, on a twentieth of an acre. I thought even if we didn't have the money, maybe we could just start looking for a new home. My argument for bigger and better would always travel full circle back to the same conclusion to stay put. If we had a larger mortgage payment and bigger bills, I would not have the option of staying home with the kids so I made our situation work.

I was washing salad greens when the phone rang. It was the doctor calling from the hospital and I immediately snapped to attention. None of Daddy's doctors called me when he was in the hospital during the past two autumns so I knew the news would be grave.

The doctor asked, "Is this Felicia Johnson?"

"Yes, this is she!" I blurted, wanting him to get right to the point.

"Your name and telephone number are in Mr. Alston's file as a next of kin. Are you a family member?"

"Yes, I am one of his two daughters."

"Well, Mr. Alston is very ill. We almost lost him last night. I would advise that you visit."

I was confused. The last time I contacted the hospital the nurse said Daddy was doing well enough to be transferred to a regular room. I guess you can't know what's going on in the hospital concerning your loved one unless you are there, and there often.

I felt a little ashamed of my ignorance of Dad's condition. I was planning to visit; I was just waiting for a time that would not put too much stress on me. There may be no need to rush after all. Last year, when he was in intensive care, the doctors said the odds of him surviving that rare attack of meningitis were not good. We rushed down there at the doctors' warning and yet, Daddy, like a real trooper, lived! I was thinking that he'd recover again.

"Yes, I am making plans to visit. What exactly is wrong?"

"He is not eating." I realized later that "not eating" may allude to a condition far worse than a lack of appetite.

The doctor continued, "He has an IV in his arm, but he must be watched. He gets confused and since the IV is probably uncomfortable, he pulls it out. He is very weak, so we are trying to give him the fluids he needs.

"What do you mean by almost lost him?"

"Last night he went into cardiac arrest. We revived him. We need to know what measures we should take, or how extensively the family wants us to work to save him if this happens again."

The doctor never directly said that Daddy died, but he probably should have to get the message through to me. I was a bit slow in processing everything I was hearing. Did Dad die? Am I suddenly the spokesperson for him and the family?

"I am not sure," I responded. "I don't think that the family wants him on a life-support system. What exactly is threatening his life?"

"We think he has bacteria in the lungs…a very aggressive form. He is undergoing several tests and if it is the form of bacteria we suspect, it will spread very rapidly and there will be no treatment against it."

I was dumbfounded. This was really bad news. Jest ten days ago, the nurse told me that Dad was moving out of ICU into a regular room, now I was practically hearing a death sentence. Suddenly I needed to see him, but I was not as free and spontaneous as I used to be. I did not want to travel now. The weather was bad, the kids were in school and I needed the income from the next few workdays since I was not paid for time off.

I knew I sounded shamefully indifferent to the person on the other end of the line. A loving daughter would have not spent any more time on the phone, but would have assured the doctor that she'd be there right away! But I had to ask more questions.

"When you say you almost lost him, do you mean that he almost died?"

"We have had to resuscitate him."

I wondered why the doctor would not say plainly that Daddy had died. What's wrong with the "D" word? I mean it is a part of life and everyone has to face it. In spite of the doctor's careful words, the cold reality hit me. Daddy had died last night. Alone. No one was with him. There were no friends and no family at his side. My heart sank. My big, strong dad died alone while his family carried on with their business. How had it come to this? Neil was living with Dad in Maryland, but was not home much of the time. My sister, who lived with Mom, was involved in her own struggles; Mom was happily remarried and working full-time. I was busy with my family. What a sad state of family affairs. What if Dad wanted someone there? What if he were afraid, lonely and depressed, although that was hard to imagine for I rarely saw that side of him. Thankfully, they had resuscitated him and he was still alive. I had a second chance to be there this time.

"We are making plans to travel down there this weekend," I offered weakly, thinking of our next convenient block of free time and feeling the doctor's disdain.

"I would get down here as soon as possible. He may not make it to the weekend."

That is not what I wanted to hear. I felt trapped, sad and angry. I felt trapped because I wanted to visit Dad, right then…but the miles and the circumstances made it so difficult. Now I regretted not going a week ago, when we all had three days off, as Irvin had suggested. I was sad because no other family member was there at his side. I was angry, feeling that Dad could have prepared me more for this.

"I understand, Doctor. I will do my best."

If Dad was dying, I hoped he had a few words to say that will fix everything before he leaves this world. I knew he expected me to handle things for him when he died. Last summer, he solemnly handed over to me a handwritten one-page last will and testament and asked me to be the executor of his estate, so I definitely needed to see him before anything happened. In accepting this responsibility, I yearned for his fatherly advice and knowledge.

With the hope that Dad would live to the weekend, I decided to leave early Thursday afternoon, so that I would miss no days of work; I had Fridays off. Irvin would miss only one day of work and the children would miss only one day of school. I wondered what condition he would be in and what he would say when I saw him. Would our relationship begin to heal? Would he finally toss empty careless words to the wind and share his heart with me? With that expectation in mind I decided the trip would be worth it.

Chapter 2

Daddy

"But the tongue can no man tame; it is an unruly evil, full of deadly poison."
James 3:8 (King James Version)

As I went through the next day, cooking, cleaning and preparing for the trip, I reflected on my relationship with my father. I could not pinpoint some happy, wonderful moment when we first connected. Mom was the center of my world when I was small, so she is the one I remembered most. My early memories of Dad are almost non-existent and I wondered how I even learned to call him "Daddy." I could only guess that as my speech and self-concept were developing, I must have learned from Mom about the man who came to and from the apartment. He was the man in our family; he belonged in our home and he was my "Daddy." He seemed always on the go with very important things to do and I did not get in his way. He came home to eat and sleep and after that, he would be gone again. He held the keys to the car, had money jingling in his pockets, knew his way around and didn't get lost or scared like me. Even though he did not interact with me, my sentiment towards him developed into one of pride and ownership. He was my dad because he was there and for a time in my life, that was enough.

We lived on the south side of Mount Vernon, a city of four square miles, on the border of New York City's most northern borough, the Bronx. On the south side of Mount Vernon, African American people were the majority. I was comfortable in my world where there were so many people with skin and hair like mine. African American people owned their own homes, businesses, stores, and held positions of leadership. We were the doctors, merchants, crossing guards and teachers. Even though I grew up in the racially turbulent sixties, I did not have to face racism as a child.

Like most working-class African Americans during that time, my parents didn't have money in stocks, savings, and other investments, but we were not poor. I thought where I lived was adequate in beauty and amenities. We lived in a thoughtfully planned low-rental community called the Levister Towers or "the projects" built in the 1950s. It consisted of several ten-story brick apartment buildings spaced out on the edge of an area the size of a few city blocks. Trees, chain-link fences, green lawns, walkways, benches and a central playground were built into the plan. It was clean and well-maintained. I had tons of fun living there because there were so many kids around and we played outside without fear. In the winter, we slid down the sloped, snow-covered lawns on sleds. In the summer we spread blankets on the grass and all year round we played tag, sidewalk games such as Girl's Are, jacks and double-dutch jump rope.

Many amenities were right there on-site or nearby. Ice cream trucks stopped right in front of my building. A soft ice cream cone cost twenty-five cents. The bookmobile stopped a short walk away. The watermelon man strolled along with his cart singing "Watermelon, man... Get your watermelon!" I could go most places I wanted to go independently—the candy store, the fish market, my cousin's house, the little dress shop where my aunts pressed dresses, the beautician's, the elementary school, and to church, which not only housed worship services, but Girl Scout meetings, and Saturday morning community programs (where I learned to crochet). I thought it was a great place for a kid to live back then.

As I thought about my childhood, I forced myself back to the task of planning for the trip ahead. I called Irvin's parents, who were retired, and as always, they were very supportive. They could watch our three children: Joel, Matthew and Marie, ages thirteen, eleven and five respectively. Mrs. Johnson even offered us the use of her car, which was a well-kept, beautiful white 1997 Toyota Camry, and we eagerly accepted. Her car was younger and classier than both of the cars we possessed—a fourteen-year-old 1987 Honda Civic and seventeen-year-old 1984 Buick Regal that my stepfather had sold to us for five hundred dollars.

I searched our files for a map of Maryland, directions and phone numbers of relatives and friends I might want to contact once we arrived at Dad's home in Riverdale. I had a cousin in Maryland, an aunt in Washington, D.C., and a friend in Alexandria, Virginia. If all went well, I might have enough time to pay them a visit.

As I packed, I searched my mind for one of my two earliest memories of Daddy. They were not very positive, but at least they gave me scenes from the past that helped me define our relationship. It took place in the living room in the year 1963. I was about four years old. Mom was in the kitchen and I was sitting comfortably on the living room coffee table, quite content and at ease. Very near to where I sat was a large cabinet-style radio/record player with double doors, big knobs and built-in speakers. I liked that piece of furniture because lots of good music flowed from it.

Though I waited for the music, I didn't remember any catchy sounds coming through this time. What I remember is Daddy. He was stooping in front of me, his face contorted with strong emotion, only inches away from mine. I held my position rigidly on the coffee table watching him intently. I had never seen his face up this close. It was interesting to observe. He was light-skinned with a broad nose and big eyes which were very expressive.

"Fulisha, git off the table!" he barked.

That must have been his first attempt ever to communicate with me. Somehow the order fell flat. He had rudely interrupted my solitary play as I was minding my own business. Besides, I hardly even knew him. If I had to translate what I felt into grown-up language, it would probably be, "You can't tell me what to do…I know your name is Daddy but I am not used to talking to you and definitely not used to taking orders from you."

I remained on the table.

"Fulisha, did you hear me? Git down off the table!" he blurted out again, showing visible impatience as his eyes grew larger.

No response from me. I was frozen in fascination that he was actually so close and speaking to me.

To his credit, instead of losing his temper, he stood up, walked towards the kitchen area and directed his words in Mom's direction, who was fixing food.

"Oh, that Fulisha…she's a stubborn one! I told her to git off the coffee table and she won' listen. She's so stubborn!"

Then he continued on his way, probably somewhere out of the apartment.

Mom always taught us to act properly so she responded to the situation by calling out to me from her spot in the kitchen.

"Felicia, get down off the coffee table."

She spoke clearly and calmly with authority. Even though my mom spent the first nineteen years of her life in a little town in Virginia, I thought it was amazing that she never acquired a southern drawl. She prided herself in the way she spoke and she never used profanity. When I heard her call out to me, I quickly responded. That voice I obeyed because it belonged to my mom who fed, clothed, and talked to me every day.

I jumped down and went about my business and exactly what that was I do not remember, but it probably was playing with toys in my room, which I did often. Dad and I didn't have another encounter again for a while.

I realized now that I was pretty much a loner when I was young. My sister, Val, was born nineteen months before me. We were close enough in age to be playmates, but there was some invisible wall that separated us and we hardly played together. It really did not bother me since Mom made sure that I had lots of books and toys to entertain myself. I spent many hours coloring pictures, playing with dolls, watching hours of TV and reading books. When I grew older, I added biking, picnicking, playing with other kids, and attending church activities to my list.

Mom made sure that we went to church. Before I turned six, I went on my own on Sunday mornings. I walked to the corner, crossed the street at the light and walked up the next block to the Baptist church. On school days, I walked one block further to the school.

In spite of my ability to find things to do, I sometimes felt sad and lonely. I just wanted to be loved, not only by my mom, but by Daddy as well. Some kids grow up desiring to be doctors, lawyers, teachers or some other worthy profession. I just wanted to be loved. My deepest childhood desire was just be a part of a happy and loving family.

The father of two girls. This was taken one month after I was born.

* * *

That evening, while questions concerning my sick father swirled inside my head, I tried to focus on my children. Joel was bouncy, friendly, very entertaining and obedient. He hardly ever got in trouble and loved to perform in front of an audience. In high school, when he was taking trumpet lessons, he'd get off the school bus and play his horn while walking home. The neighbors would applaud as the one-man parade went by their homes. Matthew was a quiet and independent thinker who liked to shock people by doing the unexpected. He was the one who flipped over the canoe on purpose when his father took him and Joel on a trip down the Delaware River. Marie was creative, sociable and fun-loving, growing up with a healthy sense of self gleaned from the abundant affection of her father and brothers. To her, any activity, whether it was swimming, dancing, making homemade videos, biking, canoeing, or eating a family meal, was always tons more fun when her brothers were around.

After dinner, I had Joel, Matt and Marie help me to clean up. I then sat down with them to tell them our plans to visit their grandfather in the hospital. Since they seldom saw my father his illness did not affect them. They were content to be going to their paternal grandparents' home. They enjoyed staying there; they were always given lots of love and attention.

The next morning, after the children were off to school, I drove to the part-time clerical job at a local lumber company. I accepted the job because the hours and commute were short: I only worked four hours a day for three days a week. This schedule afforded me time to be the mother I always desired to be. I wanted them to enjoy as many child-centered activities with Mom and/or Dad as possible which was something I always craved.

I thought about Dad as I drove down the highway, enjoying the scenic views of open space on either side of the road. The second memory I have of Daddy occurred about the same age that my own daughter fell in love with her father, sometime around age five. At that age, I too developed an interest in my father. It was then that I looked to him for acceptance and affirmation. I have never forgotten his response.

We were at home in the apartment. He was standing at a distance from me, in the front part of the apartment near the kitchen area. I stood a little further down in the hallway outside the bathroom, watching for some indication as to what I meant to him. He stared back at me and with shock and repulsion written over his face, he pronounced his assessment. Mom was nearby at the kitchen sink.

"She's funny-looking!"

He kept a safe distance away from me. The shocked glare persisted on his face a few seconds more.

I don't know what he saw at that time. Maybe Mom had not gotten around to grooming my short, coarse and kinky hair. Maybe my face was dirty. Maybe my ears stuck out too much. Whatever he saw, my dad could not get beyond it. I stood there frozen in place, not knowing what to do. He had answered my question of what he thought of me. After a moment he turned around abruptly and left. I remained in my spot a while longer, trying to figure out my next step. I felt alone. Mom was busy at the sink and did not realize what had happened.

I knew that "funny-looking" was not good by the way Dad acted. Should I then hide myself? Did this mean that he did not want me?" I did not move. I was trying to understand all of the implications of those words.

I finally processed the words as a little child would. I believed them. Daddy had spoken. I thought about the meaning of his words. I was "funny-looking." The sharp impact of the words tumbled down deep, cutting, ripping and tearing into my self-image. In the end, my spirit was not the same. If I was "funny-looking," that meant I was unlovable, and if unlovable, then worthless. His words were a deadly poison. I did not cry. Years would pass before I grieved.

I turned around towards the bedroom Valerie and I shared and numbly walked into it. I found my toys and began to play. I was safe now in solitary play. I buried the pain way deep down within and forgot all about the incident.

In those days, Mom's presence afforded me much relief. She never made me feel bad about my appearance but accepted me as I was. In her comforting presence, I could relax. In my room, I created my own world of order, beauty, love and acceptance with my Barbie dolls as long as I knew Mom was nearby. I could depend on her to not reject me. I clung to her and naturally imitated her. Mom worked hard inside and outside of the home to provide a haven for us. She was always very busy and industrious, so I stayed busy in my own little world of play, right beside her.

When Dad was not around, I could just enjoy my childhood. My favorite memories include traveling fast on foot. I loved the way I felt when I ran. When I ran, I was not defective, but powerful, free and strong. I loved running up the six flights of stairs to the apartment, to the playground, to the store, and to the many other places I was allowed to go. Often, I refused riding on the elevator just to prove to myself that I was faster than machine. I'd run down the stairways, skipping steps as I descended, then through the foyer hallway past tenants checking their mailboxes, out the front door, through the cement porch, and finally out into the bright sunshine, well before the elevator dispensed its passengers on the ground level. (I could only beat it if it stopped at several floors on the way down.) Later on, in high school, I joined the track team just to continue running. The coach urged me to take it seriously and to aim for the Olympics, but I was not interested in going the distance. I had no reason to push myself that hard.

Another of my favorite memories was in recalling how I loved twirling around in circles, with my head arched way back, making myself dizzy, looking up at the bright blue sky and clean cottony clouds. As I did this, I was made aware of another dimension. The sky was so gorgeous and its heavenly beauty made me think of the Creator. I learned about God in church. I knew that it was He who made the sun, moon, stars, clouds, animals, people and everything else in the universe. He was totally powerful and the source of all that I wanted in my life: goodness, love, truth, beauty and happiness and for some reason, I felt loved when I looked up at His celestial work. I think now that God in His wonderful love and mercy used those moments when I gazed at the sky to draw me to Himself.

One Sunday morning, with Mom's permission, I got up and left my sleeping siblings. She helped me prepare to leave the apartment to walk to church alone. Sunday school started at 9:30 a.m. She would join me later in the main service at 11:00.

Once there, I sat in the windowless Sunday school room in the church basement watching Miss Foster play the old upright piano. Its dark brown finish was dulled and scratched and the keys had yellowed. The room in which we sat was a simple square, with dreary, bare walls. We children sat on small, cold, mud-brown metal folding chairs which, though not cozy, were the perfect size for five-year-old bottoms. I tried not to let the bare skin beneath my dress touch the surface of the cold seat. There were maybe seven or eight of us children sitting attentively as we faced Miss Foster at the piano. Even as I sat on the cold, hard chair, I felt warmth in the room.

Miss Foster had friendly eyes, a gentle voice and a soft, patient smile. Her round face was framed by short hair, pressed straight, and curled tightly. Her smooth skin glistened with oil, and like many of the mothers in our church, she was pleasantly plump. She played the simple tune of "Jesus Loves Me" and taught us the words. It was a beautiful, easy song and I soaked up the lyrics like a dry sponge taking in water.

"Jesus loves me this I know,
For the Bible tells me so,
Little ones to Him belong,
We are weak but He is Strong…
Yes Jesus loves me,
Yes Jesus loves me.
Yes Jesus loves me.
The Bible tells me so."

After she taught us the lyrics, she explained that Jesus loved each and every one of us. He died on the cross to pay for our sins and wanted us to invite Him into our hearts. I wanted to be loved so much by a big strong man that I instantly and eagerly believed every word. I desperately wanted all the love Jesus could give me.

I went home and that night I said my prayers a little differently. My mom had taught me to say:

"Now I lay me down to sleep,

I pray the Lord my soul to keep,

If I die before I wake,

I pray the Lord, my soul to take."

I added something extra to that prayer that evening. Miss Foster taught us to say the prayer of a sinner. I told God that I was sorry for my sin, whatever it was. I had no idea of what I had done wrong, but if God said I was a sinner, then He was right, because He knew everything. After I apologized, I asked Jesus to come into my heart.

All of a sudden, I sensed something heavy lift off of me and then I felt so completely clean, light, and free that it was as though I had been scrubbed all over until I sparkled from the inside out. I had no idea that I was so burdened and dirty. I imagined myself being lifted up to the beautiful, gloriously blue sky in God's very own loving arms and receiving from Him a most warm and wonderful bear hug. It was such an experience that I today consider it the moment when I was born again.

After that very encouraging response to my prayer, I knew I had done the right thing, even though I could not explain any of it. God was real and Miss Foster told us all the truth. I will always remember her with special gratitude though she never knew what she did for me.

From that moment forward, there was a power present in my life to counter the negative thoughts inside my head. I had the knowledge that I was loved and accepted. I now knew someone, not just anybody, but someone, masculine, big, knowledgeable and powerful, like Dad, yet unlike Dad because he really cared. This person was greater than Daddy, Santa Claus, the Easter Bunny, the Tooth Fairy and Superman. He knew when I was sleeping; he knew when I was awake. He was invisible, so He could be with me every day and everywhere. He even knew my thoughts and the number of hairs on my head. He knew and loved me thoroughly and had lots of people worshipping and working for him, like a whole church! I was on the winning side!

Now I had a lifeboat for my sea of troubles. Now I could fix my problem with Daddy. He would not give me the attention I craved but now I had a loving heavenly Father who would, so who needed Daddy? That year, I flatly dismissed Daddy from my life and endeavored to ignore the fact that he existed as much as possible. I reasoned that it was best this way because then he could not hurt or disappoint me. It was a very neat and tidy operation which took only a second to perform. It was my solution to a big problem and I figured it should work out quite well.

I wanted to be baptized. When I told Mom, she said I was too young. So I resigned myself to wait for the day when I could show the whole church that I had accepted the Heavenly Father as my new father. Mom said to wait until I was nine years old.

In recalling this chapter of my life, I saw how I had assisted Daddy in building a wall between us. By Tuesday evening, all the plans were made for the trip. Irvin and I would leave early Thursday afternoon to arrive by the evening. I passed the next two days feeling a little guilty that I did not rush to Daddy's side, but understood that this habit began long ago. After years of pretending that he did not exist and keeping him at a safe distance, I was totally unequipped to run to him now.

I prayed for Daddy to live until the weekend.

Chapter 3

Someone to Love

"A new commandment I give unto you, that you love one another; as I have loved you, that ye also love one another."
John 13:34 (King James Version)

Looking back was definitely helping to explain my present family predicament so I continued. I thought back again, this time to May of 1964. I had just turned five and my mom disappeared suddenly. I looked for her all throughout our five-room apartment to no avail. I could not find my mother and I felt lost and forsaken without her.

I did find someone else, however. There was a strange little elderly lady, moving silently about in the kitchen. She had soft salt-pepper hair tied into a bun. Her skin was honey brown like Mom's, but her body was shorter and wider. Her dress was dreary to look at. It had no captivating shapes, patterns or colors. She was very quiet. It annoyed me to see her fooling around with my mom's pots and pans. I didn't know who she was and didn't trust her. I watched her closely and followed every move of her hands—from the sink to the shelves to the stove top and back to the sink. What was she doing? She was messing with my mom's things and she did not put them back where they belonged. Obviously, she didn't know what she was doing and needed my help. She was lifting up a pot to put it away.

"That doesn't go there," I stated, protecting my mom's kitchen procedures.
She did not respond.

"That goes there," I corrected again. I was already offended that she was there in my mom's place. I was not about to let her just take over and change my beloved's way of doing things.

Years later, I smiled as Mom explained my grandmother's reaction to my "help." Before leaving, Grandma Fields, who was somewhat amused at her irritating five-year-old granddaughter, teasingly announced to Mom, "I'm so glad you're home and now I can leave…'cause that chil' of yours kept following me around in the kitchen, telling me where you kept everything. If I put something in the wrong place she would tell me, 'My mom don't keep it there.' So I am so glad you are back and that I am going home!"

I had no idea that she was my mother's mother and that she was seething inside as I helped her. She seemed so tranquil at the time. When I finally got to know her, Grandma impressed me as a very gentle person. I never heard her complain or talk negatively about anyone and she was always calm and patient with me.

That event is the only thing I remembered about Grandmother's visit and before I knew it, Mom was back home and Grandma gone. But, I was in for another surprise. When Mom came home she brought an intruder with her— a definite unwanted guest on my list. In the days to follow, I watched this uninvited guest suspiciously from the doorway of Mom's bedroom, not venturing to enter.

I didn't understand why she was giving so much attention to that strange, doll-size creature. My doll babies didn't take that much time to care for. I could leave them for days if I wanted to. So why did this thing take so much of my mom's attention? I used to spend hours beside her, imitating her as she washed and ironed the clothes, cooked the meals and cleaned the apartment. We were very content working side by side. Ever since she brought this doll-thing home and was always fiddling with it, I did not know where I fit in anymore.

One day, I just stood in her doorway, feeling completely forsaken. Mom held the thing in her arms and kept looking down at it. She didn't notice me. I drifted away to my room and my toys. I decided that I'll just have to inspect that doll-thing on my own, when I get the chance, to see why it mesmerized my mom all day long.

The opportunity arose one day when I found the doll-thing alone in my parents' bedroom, lying in a crib. The sun's rays poured brightly through the window illuminating the soft blue walls. I looked up at the window and saw the chimney stacks of a nearby tower building, clouds and blue sky. I tiptoed towards the crib, nervously, not knowing what to expect. Everything was quiet, including the thing in the crib. In spite of my fear, curiosity drove me closer and closer to that unfamiliar piece of furniture that reminded me of a zoo cage painted white. When I reached it, I looked through the bars and saw the doll-thing up close. It was still, quiet and doing nothing. It was just lying on its back, practically bald and wrapped in dull colors. Its eyes were closed in the middle of a bright day. How boring! Why all the fascination over something so colorless that just lies there! I was not impressed! I wondered what purpose it served other than to take my mom from me.

I had to give it a little pain for the discomfort it brought into my life. I reached out. My small hand easily slipped in between the crib bars. My right thumb and forefinger were poised to execute the necessary catalyst for revenge which in my book was a good pinch! That ought to make it sorry. Then I'll observe the response and snicker over my ability to make it unhappy. Yet, because I didn't know its powers, I had to move with caution. Slowly, my hand reached toward a bare leg. The fat part of the leg looks like a good target...closer, closer...almost there...

"Felicia, what are you doing?" Mom asked suddenly as she entered the room.

I jolted back, feeling guilty and ashamed. Of course, I could not explain my actions. I sulked away to my toys in my room. That was one pinch that never happened.

I did not belong anymore. Daddy didn't want me and was hardly around. My big sister, Valerie, was always out playing with other people, and now Mom is too busy with this invader to notice me. I was lonelier than ever.

Years later Mom told me that my behavior disturbed her. She confided in an older lady about the problem she was having with me. She explained to the sympathetic older woman that her five-year-old had become withdrawn and quiet since the baby came. The lady wisely gave her a very simple piece of advice. She told Mom to include me in caring for the baby.

A few days after speaking with the elderly lady, Mom was sitting with it in her lap again. I was dismally watching her from the doorway when she called me over and asked me to help her care for the baby. She taught me how to put on his clothes and to hold him in my lap. When she bathed and dressed it, she needed me to pass her the washcloth, baby soap and towel. I was elated! My mom included me in her life again.

From that day forward, the thing was a baby and the baby had a name. Neil was my little brother. I helped care for him and loved him as my own. When he began to walk and run, we had so much fun. Our favorite game was a tickling game that I called the "koo-koo test."

"It's time for the koo-koo test!" I exclaimed.

Upon that announcement, he would start giggling in anticipation and make haste to run away, his short toddler legs going up and down as fast as they could. I would easily catch him, put him on the bed or couch and proceed to tickle his stomach until he doubled over in laughter. I was surprised at how easy it was to make him laugh. If my finger only touched a rib, he'd collapse in a wave of uncontrollable giggles. Thus, I thought this game was excellently named for it measured his level of "koo-koo-ness," which was definitely off the charts.

He laughed also when I mashed in the faces of my toy rubber mice, Ellen and Andy. They came to me with a treehouse equipped with a swing one Christmas morning. (I told Mom that I wanted it when I saw it advertised on TV.) Sometimes, I'd make my pink rubber mice put on a show for Neil. During the "Ellen and Andy Show," Neil would crack up as I distorted their soft faces; pushing them in with my thumb to make their eyes touch. These mice were amazing. They could sing and dance and even make me laugh.

I liked helping to care for my brother; it made me feel needed. On a regular basis, whenever I prepared a bowl of cereal for myself such as on a Saturday morning, I would also fix one for him. Then we'd sit down on the living room floor and watch the Saturday morning cartoons while eating several bowls of Sugar Pops and Frosted Flakes.

There were times, however, when all I could do was to stand by helplessly and watch. I think some scary new experiences were meant for a father to handle such as the time when I saw my little brother's unexplainable agony when he, Mom and I got caught in the rain. We were walking back to our apartment building from the stores when raindrops began to fall. Perhaps it was his first experience being exposed to rain on an uncovered, freshly shaven head at the age of two. Maybe he was just a little boy who just needed his daddy's presence to feel brave. I don't know the reason, but as the rain began, Neil panicked and frantically wiped off the first drop that landed on his head. Another drop hit his ear; he quickly wiped that one off. More rain began to hit him three and four drops at a time. By then he was hysterical, crying, prancing about and slapping his head to fend off the drops. It was a good thing we were only a few yards from the building entrance when it began to pour.

In regards to my sister, Valerie, I don't remember her much before my adolescent years. She was more popular than I. She possessed an outgoing personality and was very attractive. Her very cute face was framed with softer, less kinky, jet black hair. She had small shapely lips and her dreamingly attractive eyes were never obscured by glasses. She was often out spending her time socializing with relatives or friends. Since I did not fit into her world, I concentrated my energy on caring for Neil as long as I could, for I thoroughly enjoyed having someone to love.

Chapter 4

Grade School

"For God hath not given us the spirit of fear; but of power, and of love, and of a sound mind."
2 Timothy 1:7 (King James Version)

It was upsetting thinking of Daddy dying all alone. This was not how things were supposed to be. He had three children who loved him. I wanted all of us, even Mom, to surround him with love and support. Realistically, however, I wouldn't even be at his side until Thursday and who knew how much good that would do. The ugly truth stared me in the face. My family had an abundance of disconnections.

While the present circumstances looked grim, the future looked worse. Rather than think of either, I roamed about in the certainty of my past, reliving pleasant memories and finding helpful bits of understanding that answered some of the questions popping in my head. Why didn't Dad need us as he lay for weeks in the hospital? What happened to our family's unity? Did we ever possess such a thing? Something beautiful and unexpected happened when I reflected back. I remembered the many ways throughout my life when the Lord was there, directing, blessing and sustaining me. In facing the trials ahead, I encouraged myself by remembering.

To jar my memory, I went into our bedroom and searched through my personal records in the file cabinet. In some old school folders, I found report cards from elementary school. I read one from kindergarten as I sat on the carpet with my back against the wall.

I remembered that God even blessed my first experience with school. Upon arriving at school the first day, I felt brave since Mom and I had visited the teacher and my classroom the day before. I sat at one of the long, rectangular tables, which seated eight children, I think. I didn't talk much the first few days because I needed time to observe my new surroundings and peers, but when I realized that no one called me derogatory names, I began to relax and enjoy my new environment.

Kindergarten was filled with fun and stimulating activities. What thrilled me most was the fact that the adults spent time with us children. We were the center of their world. They read to us, sang songs to us and taught us for hours on end.

I thought of my kindergarten teacher. She was a stout woman with soft curls adorning her round, pretty face. She wore brightly colored floral blouses and dresses. Her eyes were a little slanted and her skin was the color of honey. She reminded me of the Hawaiian people I saw on television. She smiled easily but was definitely the one in charge.

One day during art time, when we were told to draw an animal, I cut out a three-dimensional paper lion that could stand on its four legs. His head was made from a round, separate piece of paper, which I attached to his body by cutting little slits in the paper. My teacher got all excited and ran out the room to the neighboring teachers bragging about my work. I was surprised and elated! My self-worth increased several notches that day, and throughout my days in school, I did my best to repeat that euphoria of praise over and over again. God's gift of a sound mind was a tremendous blessing for I needed all the help I could get.

I ran all the way home, feeling proud of myself. School work and running made me feel valuable, capable and gifted. So I worked hard for good grades and ran practically everywhere I went.

Dad didn't understand me. In fact, once or twice, when Dad saw me running, he flat out told me to stop. It's true that when I ran, sometimes I fell, skinned my knee and bawled as though I was going to die, but he was not the one who bandaged up my wound. Still he ordered me to stop.

"Fulisha, stop that running! Can't you go somewhere without running? Walk!"

I walked while he was within sight, but took off running when I knew he could not see me. Since he was rarely outside with me, I ran a lot. He just did not understand. He didn't know me. He didn't know that running made me feel perfected.

* * *

Mom noticed my speech one day. "I can wun fast!"
She answered back,
"Tie your shoelaces!"
"Okay, I can tie my sues all by myself!"
The sounds made by the letters "r" and "sh" were not formed by these lips. But unlike the cartoon character Elmer Fudd on television, I had a wise teacher who cared enough to recommend that I see a speech therapist. Of course, Mom agreed to any service that would help me excel, so the therapy sessions were arranged right there at the school.

I was pulled out of the classroom a few times a week to see the therapist. All I can remember about this lady was her mouth. As she put her face directly in front of mine, she told me to watch her lips and then, very slowly, she pronounced the sounds I could not articulate. I watched her exaggerated tongue and lip movements over and over until finally, one day I was able to imitate them. What euphoria I experienced when it all clicked and I was able to pronounce the "sh" and "rrr" sounds. I don't think I even thanked that lady.

I moved on to first grade and fell in love with a boy. He was the color of coffee with one drop of cream, and he flashed large, dark eyes set in a perfectly round head with a glaze of black velvet fur on top. He had a beautiful grin. I thought he was *so* handsome.

He reminded me of Flip Wilson, an African American television comedian in the sixties, who made me laugh when I watched his program, *The Flip Wilson Show*. I think he must have been the first African American man I saw regularly on our television, which produced only black-and-white pictures. I figured if Flip Wilson could make me laugh, he must be nice and if I were older, I would write him a letter. Since he was out of my reach, I turned my attention to a look-alike, who was there before me in flesh and blood.

This kid never knew how much I adored him. When he spoke to me, I was speechless. I simply froze, stunned by his interest and too afraid to move, lest I do something to frighten him away. I was not used to such attention. So I did what came naturally to me at that time when I was noticed for my outward appearance: I shut down, like a frightened roly-poly bug, curling up into a tight ball after it has been touched.

One day as I started walking home from school, the love of my life approached me. Grinning from ear to ear and with a confident step, he asked to carry my things as we walked home. Hardly looking him in the eye, I handed him my load of books and a lunch box. He carried them a few yards to the corner, and then gave them back to me, smiling exuberantly. My heart melted. What a dream! I turned to walk in the direction of my home, thinking I must definitely marry that boy! After that incident, he faded from my life, but he left me with the impression that at least for a moment, I was lovable.

In the midst of blissful elementary school days was increasing disorder at home. One evening, while I was playing in the room my sister and I shared, I anxiously listened to Mom and Dad's rising voices. Then I heard Mom moving quickly and clumsily through the apartment towards me. She knocked into the dresser as she rushed into a corner. Her right arm was up shielding her face as she ducked. An iron flew across the room and smashed into the wall. Daddy glared in the doorway, his eyes bulging and his face reddened with fury.

"You say another word to me and I'll knock you clear out of here! You hear me, woman! Just keep talking!

Mom fearfully stared back from her huddled position in silence.

Dad stormed out. Mom went to her room, sat on her bed and began to cry quietly, dabbing her eyes with tissues. I stood at her doorway watching. She was all I had. Now, she was hurting. What do you do when your angel cries?

I continued watching her from the entrance. I felt so glum and sad. As I watched her sitting on the edge of her bed, looking down at her lap, sobbing and wiping her face, tears fell freely down my cheeks. I returned to my room where I could cry privately. I kept listening for cues from Mom. I couldn't stop crying until she did. She eventually got up and washed her face, then went back to her household chores. I don't think she noticed me in her intense pain. She didn't need to. I just needed to know that she was okay, and when I thought she was, I went back to playing.

I cried a lot with Mom in those early years.

* * *

School continued to be a welcomed change from the isolation and anxiety at home. In second grade the kids were friendly and receptive and the work was fun and easy.

My second-grade teacher was younger than my first two teachers. She looked like one of those Caucasian pretty, teenaged actresses I watched on television. Like many teachers in the day when penmanship was important, she wrote with beautiful handwriting in the teacher's comment section of my progress report. In the first quarterly period ending in November, she wrote:

"Felicia is a quiet child and very diligent about her work. She shows wonderful creativity in her work. Her behavior is pleasant. Although she does not participate very often in class discussions, she grasps new ideas readily."

I was a serious and productive worker, like Mom. In January, she wrote:

"Felicia is still progressing in second grade and is doing very well. She is very friendly and well liked by her classmates."

I was relaxed, feeling accepted and competent. I loved people and enjoyed socializing. But, by April, I was beginning to annoy her. She wrote:

"Felicia is becoming very social minded and allows this to distract her in class. She completes her written work only to have time to converse with her friends. She does not remain in her seat as she should."

I don't remember any such rule. I was having a ball. Nobody was rejecting me and I finally had friends!

By June 23, 1967, my teacher was feeling upbeat and gracious…school was over and summer vacation had arrived. She wrote:

"Felicia's work has been excellent this year. It was a pleasure to have her in class."

I saw God's hand in my love for school and in providing teachers who encouraged me. It was a place where I could learn and enjoy positive feedback from the adult world when I needed it most.

Chapter 5

Baptism

"Come unto me, all ye that labour and are heavy laden, and I will give you rest. Take my yoke upon you, and learn of me; for I am meek and lowly in heart: and ye shall find rest unto your souls. For my yoke is easy, and my burden is light."

Matthew 11:28-30 (King James Version)

Third grade passed without any major incident except that in the last marking period, I turned nine years old and I had waited long enough. I was ready to prove to anyone interested that I had a new Father, the Great Creator God and Savior of the World, Jesus Christ. It was time to be baptized!

This event took place in front of the church, which had a baptismal pool under the raised platform which supported the pulpit and choir seats. A door was lifted up to reveal a small rectangular pool, filled with about three feet of water. I was one of a group of women being baptized, and we were all dressed in long, white, cotton robes that spread out like tents and bathing caps that covered hot-combed hair. The number of men being baptized was much smaller, and they formed a group behind us.

The choir, dressed in their gloriously shiny robes, sitting behind the pulpit in the semicircular choir seats, sang slowly and solemnly:

Take me to the waters,
Take me to the waters,
Take me to the waters,
To be baptized.

I love Jesus,
I love Jesus,
I love Jesus,
Yes, I do.

After watching the women ahead of me get soaked, I saw the signal that it was my turn. I obediently moved forward. Two elderly deacons, standing on either side of me, held my elbows as I descended the steps leading into the pool. As I stood rigidly in the pool, the cold water rested at my waist causing me to shiver. My swimming cap was too tight and probably cutting off blood flow to my brain. My thick-lens glasses were being held by a church staff member so everything I saw was blurry. I thought that this should be a spiritual moment, when I should hear heavenly voices and see visions, so I tried hard to think of Jesus, even though I was not liking the idea of being tipped backwards into the frigid water by strangers and possibly getting my hair wet 'cause those caps don't always work. The pastor and a deacon tightened their grip on me. It was time. I tensed up.

Pastor, lifting his head, bellowed so the whole church could hear:

"Sister, have you accepted Jesus Christ as your personal Lord and Savior?"

I nodded and a faint "yes" must have escaped from my lips for the pastor was satisfied and he continued on.

"Then, by the authority vested in me, I baptize you, my sister, in the name of the Father, the Son and of the Holy Ghost."

With sudden force, Pastor placed a white folded cloth over my nose and then, in perfect unison, he and the deacon dipped me backward beneath the surface of the water. My eyes were tightly shut and I held my breath. Before I could panic, I was standing on my feet again, reeling from the weight of soaking wet clothing.

I felt like a mess but strong arms supported me as I clumsily made my way out of the pool. Someone thoughtfully draped me with a large dry towel and directed me to follow the water-logged path of the others to the restrooms in the church basement below. I may have been born again on the inside, but I was still living in my body and felt every bit of its weight.

Maybe the experience would have been more glorious if I were baptized in the beautiful Jordan River or the Sea of Galilee on a warm sunny day, where I could look up into the sky, like they did in the Bible. Then again, I may have recoiled at the sharp rocks and smelly fish.

I was now an official church member and able to get involved in activities. I participated in the annual Christmas pageant and joined the youth choir. I attended rehearsals, summer carnivals and dozens of fund-raising social teas. At these food socials, we studious and "nerdy" kids would entertain the adults by reciting Christmas, Easter or Mother's Day poems and singing solos and then reward ourselves at the long banquet tables.

God had to teach me a lesson about gluttony. I made a habit of stuffing myself by sampling as many of the homemade dishes prepared by the numerous church mothers that appealed to me. One time I ate four types of meat (fried chicken, honey glazed ham, roast beef and fried fish) two different vegetables (collard greens, green beans), five different starches (macaroni and cheese, potato salad, corn bread, stuffing and sweet potatoes) and five desserts (a cupcake, a slice of chocolate layer cake, a slice of apple pie, one piece of sweet potato pie, and a brownie) all at one time. The next morning I felt terrible pain in my stomach, of such intensity I had never experienced, before or since. I cried out to God, pleading with Him to forgive me and to let me live as I sat bent over on the toilet seat. After what seemed like hours, my body succeeded in purging out the toxic mixture and I found relief. I was very thankful that the Lord spared my life. After that, I used more self-control at food gatherings.

I enjoyed attending the main worship service for three reasons. First, there was a sense of beauty, unity, and order in worshipping God that I loved. Secondly, Mom was usually there with me. The third reason was that it was very interesting watching the adults. Sometimes the preacher became animated as he delivered his soulful monologue, punctuated by perfectly timed "Amen's" and "Yes, Lord!'s" from the deacon's bench and stirring musical chords from the organist. When the atmosphere was pregnant with emotion, I knew to keep my eye on one particular deacon, who was light-skinned with shiny wavy hair. He would shout out loud in a high-pitched voice, grab his side with his hand, double over, stomp a few times, then arch backward and shriek, "Jesus!" right down in front of the whole church. I wondered how anyone had the courage to command all that attention. I concluded that it must be God's Spirit moving him, because nobody could have that much nerve.

If it was a long boring service and I was sitting next to Mom, I usually ended up annoying her by fidgeting or falling asleep slumped against her. She would nudge me with her arm and give me chewing gum to perk me up, but the flavor only lasted a few minutes. Church was two hours.

Becoming a member of the youth choir solved the boredom problem. The four-part harmonies were intriguing and I learned many inspiring songs. Quite a few of the songs we performed were the works of the Edwin Hawkin Singers such as "I Heard The Voice of Jesus Say," and "Come and Go With Me to My Father's House." Thankfully, the choir was pretty active during the service so I could not fall asleep. We first marched into the sanctuary from the rear, up the aisle, singing and stepping to the beat of the music. Once at the front, we sat down in unison on padded choir benches behind the pulpit, facing the congregation. Throughout the service we stood up several times to sing a song or a refrain. From my seat, I could always spy several sleeping adults among the congregation. I tried especially hard to set a good example by sitting erectly and staying alert—although if the service dragged on I, along with an increasing number of other choir members, would succumb to slouching, passing notes and feasting on candies.

* * *

As I entered adolescence, I no longer had to wonder why I needed to be saved. I learned soon enough that I was filled with all sorts of evil desires that just popped up from heaven knows where. Mom was too busy working to see the depth of my depravity and Dad was not around, but the Lord was there to rescue me from myself. He filled in the gap and disciplined me better than ten thousand parents.

I used to steal quarters out of my mother's pocketbook, which I would sneak into the bathroom with me. When I got the quarters, I'd put them in my shorts pocket and run down the six flights to exit the building as quickly as possible. Once outside, I'd buy myself, and any available friend, Mr. Softly ice cream cones. My favorite was chocolate. God stopped that practice. Once I read the scriptures on stealing, I lost the desire to continue on with my little self-made funding program. God's Word worked when my mother's spanking had no effect.

The strong arm of the Lord corrected me again during those elementary school years, when I was drawn into a form of play in which we unsupervised children played "house" by kissing and rubbing against each other. One day, as I was lying down, I felt the strong Presence of the Holy Spirit hover over me. I got a very strong impression that what I was about to do would greatly displease Him and I froze in place. Without any words spoken, I knew the Lord's Spirit was pleading with me to not proceed with my plan of action. Instead of feeling rebellious and angry, I felt actually honored that He cared enough to stop me from doing something that He did not like. I yielded to God's Spirit, got up without a word of explanation and went directly to the bathroom. As I sat alone, the heavy Spirit of the conviction lifted and I felt such an immediate sense of liberation, victory and joy that I almost laughed out loud. I was astonished that obedience to His revealed will could bring such sheer happiness. I knew from that incident that I could trust Him to help me make the right choices as I floundered about in life, without my daddy's direction.

Chapter 6

Mom's People

"A godly life brings huge profits to people who are content with what they have."
1 Timothy 6 (GOD'S WORD)

To an outsider, our family probably appeared to be faring well. None of us were drug addicts, alcoholics or criminals. We had no chronic diseases, major catastrophes, or financial hardships. My parents were both respectable citizens, holding long-term jobs, and Dad paid the rent every month. We wore new clothes every season and had adequate food supplies in the cupboard, felt the heat emanating from the painted radiators, and enjoyed luxuries such as the television, telephone, and electricity in the wall sockets. We were rich compared to some people.

We even had summer vacations. Our accommodations were not at luxury hotels or fancy resorts, but in the warm cozy homes of our parents' parents. Mom and Dad were both diligent in returning to their childhood homes every summer, and because of this, I got to see my grandmothers each summer for a period of about eight years. The visits made up my most pleasant family memories. They were capsules of happy, though sometimes extremely boring times in the country, and through them I learned to appreciate both my relatives and the more quiet and rustic side of life.

Those trips sparked my interest in my grandmother's history. She, my mother and my aunts did not mind sharing their stories. Grandmother had already been married and widowed before she met my mother's father, John Fields. She married Matthew Taylor when she was about twenty years old and gave birth to nine children, one every two years starting in 1916. The seven in order of birth were Margaret, James, Arthur, Helen, Robert, Mary, and Rosa, Thomas and Susy. In 1920, Grandmother sacrificially relinquished her third child and infant son, Arthur, to her sister Carrie who was childless. While she was pregnant with her fourth, she became so sick that she nearly died. The doctor scolded Grandpa Taylor and warned him to not neglect his wife's physical needs. She was dehydrated, severely exhausted and suffering from poor nutrition. She recovered, giving birth to a healthy baby girl, Helen, in 1922. Over the next ten years, five more were born: Robert in 1924, Mary in 1926, Rosa in 1928, Thomas in 1930 and Susy in 1932.

Some time during in the early 1930s, Mr. Taylor died. He was sick with what they called "catarrh," which is similar to a severe head cold only worse, resulting in the swelling of mucous membranes in the throat and nose area, which I imagine would cause serious complications if the inflammation blocked the air or food passages. Aunt Mary told me what she could recall about her father. Her only memory of him occurred when she was three years old. She watched him as he prepared to leave the yard to go into a field. They were standing by a big tree when he called out to his son Robert, "Come on. I'm gonna take you with me." Aunt Mary cried out, "Daddy, take me!" She was hurt by his reply, "No, you're too little; go back into the house." She didn't get to accompany her father that time, but the day before he died, she got up on the bed where he lay and snuggled up against him.

Grandmother was soon alone caring for eight children in a small two-bedroom wooden house deep in the woods. Life became extremely difficult. The eldest children found work. Aunt Margaret did domestic chores and Uncle James found employment working on a farm, but there were still six children who needed constant care. Sometime around 1933, Grandmother decided that she would have to work outside the home in order to meet her family's continuous needs. She asked family members to help her, and they responded by taking her six children into their homes so that she could find work. Grandmother's brother, Arthur, and his wife traveled many miles to bring eleven-year-old Helen and seven-year-old Mary back with them to Cleveland, Ohio. They took Helen, but Aunt Mary refused to go, telling them "I don't wanna go…I'm not going." She could not bear the thought of leaving her mother. She was sent instead to live with her maternal grandfather, William Mikeal, whose home was within walking distance to her mother's.

Soon, Great-Grandfather Mikeal moved Grandmother Fields out of the house in the woods to a better place. From her new circumstances and most likely with the pain of a broken heart from having to part with so many of her children, she found work caring for four children of a white couple in town. Many years later, one of the sons of this family became the doctor who helped Grandmother gain admittance to a local nursing home when she had no financial assets, saying that she took care of him when he was young, now it was his turn to do what he could for her.

Within a year of finding work in town, Grandmother met and married my grandfather, John Fields. I always wanted to know the wonderfully warm and loving man who was my mother's father, so I asked more questions and found out that at the time he met my grandmother, he was a cotton picker struggling to provide for five children, three of which still lived at home. The marriage was a blessing as these two people with deep losses found comfort in each other. John Fields was also widowed with children ranging from ages nine to twenty. He and his first wife, Betty, produced five children: Mollie, Edgar, Bernie, Anne and Freddie.

Change was in the wind. Grandmother Fields told her new husband, "I'm not picking nobody's cotton." Soon afterwards Grandpa Fields found work as a tobacco sharecropper, moving to the first of a series of tenant houses owned by landowners. Meanwhile, Aunt Mary was miserable at her grandparents' house. Many days after school, she would sit on the porch and cry. Her Grandfather Mikeal inquired as to why that child was crying. He was told that she missed her mother. He then instructed his teenage son to escort Aunt Mary back to see her mother on several occasions.

The day came when Grandmother Fields decided to talk to her husband about her children. He replied that he could only take in two of her children. The two chosen were Mary and Rosa. After being away for two years, Aunt Mary was happy to finally be at her mother's side again. She didn't mind that she had no place to sleep except at her parents' feet. She told me that Mr. John Fields was the only father she ever knew.

Grandmother Fields was in her early forties when she gave birth to the last two daughters of John Fields, my mother, Marie, and her sister Lucille. They were precious and adored by their older parents who had found a second chance at love. The middle-aged parents expected their daughters to be kind and decent, to be involved in church, and to make good grades in school. When the sisters played, they drew in the dirt, rode bikes and dressed their big, white, hard plastic dolls. Their chores included milking the cow and helping their mother in the garden.

Aunt Lucille wondered why her mother even bothered with the hard work of growing one's own food. She felt that there was hardly anything worthwhile growing in the garden except for green beans and sweet potatoes. Why take the trouble to milk the cow, when its milk was "nasty" because it had been chewing on green onions? Why worry with canning vegetables when Daddy is willing to drive to the store to get the best food in the world—pork and beans and hot dogs! Today, Aunt Lucille loves fresh garden vegetables, but never did quite develop a taste for butter.

By Mom's own account, her father was a caring and gentle man who was good to his wife and children. Just as he'd go to the store for frank and beans for Aunt Lucille, he thought nothing of walking a mile just to get my mom bananas to put in her cereal.

According to what Mom told me, her father died on Friday, February 12, 1954, five years before I was born. He had been diagnosed with heart problems and needed to sit up with his head propped up by pillows in order to breathe at night. She used to listen to her father's wheezing at night.

Somehow, shortly before he died, she sensed his premonition of death. She explained that in January they had just moved into the newly erected cinder-block house, which her father paid to have built for his family. In the next few weeks, he worked so feverishly around the house trying to complete the finishing touches that Grandmother Georgia Fields admonished him to slow down. Mom remembered his reply, "I want to get the house ready for you and the children, even if I don't live in it."

Mom also thought it odd on the day he died that he dressed differently. He wore a white shirt that was opened at the neck; he usually buttoned his shirt all the way up to keep out the winter chill. That very morning, she prepared to drive him to the doctor's office for a checkup and expected him to start the car up and maneuver it into position for her to drive out of the yard. Instead, he directed her to turn the car around, saying, "You might as well learn to do it." Mom did learn to maneuver that car around that day, just as she learned to submit the bill payments and drive her parents and little sister on countless errands months before. On this day, when her dad delegated even more responsibility to her, she suspected that he knew his time was short in spite of the doctor's good report.

That evening, Grandmother Fields and Aunt Lucille had gone to bed. My mother stayed up to assist her father after he had finished watching a boxing match on television with Uncle Thomas. When it was finished, Uncle Thomas left for his house in town. Once the television was turned off, Mom helped her father turn down the kerosene heater for the night and then she began to walk into the bedroom. Before she reached the doorway, she heard her father suddenly call out, "Georgia! Georgia! Georgia!"

Mom turned around and ran back to her father as he slid down off the chair. His color had grayed by the time he was on the floor. Mother screamed out to awake her mother then frantically ran through the field to a relative's house in the total darkness. She still has a scar on her knee to mark where she fell on a rock. Her father was cold by the time she returned with her half brother, Bernie, and his wife, Edmonia, panting behind her.

Grandfather died that February and Mom spent the following months mourning deeply, crying often, and wishing to have her father back. She missed him intensely. As long as she could remember, he was always there. When she was little, she'd bring him his slippers which were almost too heavy for her to carry. He lavished her with love and attention, sitting her on his knees, telling her folktales, filling her heart with laughter and her belly with soda pops, cheese, peanut butter and, of course, bananas. When she grew older, he was there driving her and Aunt Lucille to and from school, giving her money from his pockets and inspiring her to be capable, resourceful and independent.

While the pain of her father's passing was still intense, Mom finished her studies and graduated from high school in June 1954. She moved to New York at the urging of her sisters, with hopes of enrolling in a business school. Aunt Mary offered her the vacant room in her apartment, which was recently occupied by her brother-in-law and my dad, Cornelius. He came back around often to visit and the stage was set for him and my mom to meet and eventually marry.

* * *

Though barely, that house that Grandpa Fields built still stands. It's vacant and deteriorating. It is deeded to all of the heirs of John Fields, which makes it impossible to sell since one heir cannot be located. I remember it as it used to be in 1960s and 1970s, maintained and full of life. Woods bordered one side of the house and on the other side were lawn chairs under two tall trees. In the backyard were a vegetable garden, the wood pile, a clothesline strung between trees near a wooden table used for doing laundry and a foot path trailing to the outhouse. The front yard provided a great space for running around in circles and playing tag and was ornamented by small shrubs and two flowerbeds. The house had a simple square floor plan, divided into four rooms: a bedroom, a living room, dining room and a kitchen. The upper level had two rooms. There was no basement, garage, central air, central heating system, or indoor plumbing.

I was entranced by both the beauty and ruggedness of life at my Grandmother Fields' home. If you wanted water, you worked for it. Grandma had a water pump just outside the back door. We filled up tin buckets and basins with water for washing and cooking. If you wanted hot water, you worked a little harder. We heated the water on the wood-burning stove after building a strong fire. Uncle James, the eldest son who lived in a room upstairs, cut the wood over at the woodpile and loaded it into a big wooden box in the kitchen. That box was not only the home to the wood, but to an ever-multiplying colony of the most detestable insect I ever encountered—roaches. Thankfully, in the years to come, my aunts helped Grandmother get rid of the box and its tenants by installing an electric oven as well as a sink with running water. We still had to heat the water, but it was a lot easier to do with electricity than wood.

The outhouse was a narrow, unpainted wooden structure at the end of a worn path lined by thick, tall weeds that probably hid snakes. If you were an adult and had to use the outhouse at night, your only guide through the intense darkness was a flashlight with a weak battery. We children were spared that ordeal and could take care of our business in the comfort of the bedroom, in a metal chamber pot. Of course, once we were old enough, we emptied our own pot or used the outhouse. Once, when I mustered enough courage to look down the smelly hole in the ground, I was surprised to see hundreds of white worms or maggots wiggling in the putrid murkiness below. I thought it awfully clever of God to devise a way to dispose of that stuff by making it so palatable to another creature.

Of the two rooms in the attic, one was used for storage and the other belonged to Uncle James. That part of the house to me was uninviting—dreary and bare. I know, because I ventured up there a few times but did no more than glance around quickly. The light from two windows illuminated the piles of dirty clothes, a twin-size iron-frame bed, a few rough wooden crates and an unfinished wooden floor. As I looked around, the strong odors of smoke, sweat and dust stung my nose. Within minutes, I ran back down the stairs into Grandma's brightly lit, welcoming, yellow kitchen.

In spite of his living quarters, Uncle James was special. While Daddy dropped us off at the house and then sped off, destination unknown, Uncle James spent time with me. I looked to this gentle man for laughs, entertainment and affirmation because he rarely let me down. He hardly bathed, but his odor didn't repel me. I think we were both just glad to be accepted by one another. The clothes he wore were stained and tattered, his body was way too thin, his skin was prematurely wrinkled, and he talked a little funny for lack of a few front teeth, but I was enthralled by the attention he gave to me. Indoors, we played lots of bingo games at the dining room table. I liked it best when we sat outside under the trees and together observed busy ants dragging food crumbs and dead insects to their underground nests. He told me riddles and showed me tricks he could do with his fingers, separating them one, two, and three at a time. Sometimes, I just watched him work as he mowed the grass and cut wood. Afterwards, he'd sit at the dining room table waiting for a meal, with his thin legs crossed, cigarette hanging from his lips, and bending forward a little to look out the window. When I saw him looking out the window I sometimes wondered about his hopes and dreams.

He never told me about himself and I never asked. Years after he died, I learned from Aunt Mary that he fell when washing windows at a school in Arlington, and that perhaps the injuries from the fall combined with his drinking habit caused him to develop seizures. I knew that on occasion he did not come home and instead was found somewhere in a drunken stupor, even in a ditch along the road. Eventually, he was placed in a special home several hours far out in the country where he could not find his way back to a liquor store. I visited him shortly before he died at the age of sixty-eight in 1986. With the guidance of Uncle Thomas, my fiancé and I drove out to where Uncle James was residing. I don't think he remembered me as I sat beside him on a step so low we were practically in the dirt. He looked more haggard and even more emaciated than I remembered, but he seemed happy as he grinned toothlessly and rambled on. I didn't understand a word he said, but I went away feeling that by visiting him I had in some way thanked my dear Uncle James.

It was always more fun when our cousins joined us at Grandma's in the summer. Aunt Margaret had a daughter almost my age. They lived a few blocks away from us in Mount Vernon. Darlene was like a sister to me. We played well together. We could just look at each other and burst out laughing, hilariously, at absolutely nothing. We found it very hard to be serious. My Aunt Lucille had three daughters; a son was born later. We girls had fun dressing up, sprinkling our bosoms with powder, spraying the perfume and filling up our pocketbooks as we prepared for church or for going into town.

One especially hot day, one of the adults must have either gotten tired of sticky, sweaty children running around, or must have known how miserably hot we were for she got out the hose and filled a couple of large tin washbasins with cold water right outside the back door. She added a few gallons of hot water from the kettle and pots, then gave us soap, towel and a washcloth. I stripped down to pure skin right there in the great outdoors. Looking down at my chest, I felt justified; it looked just like a boy's. I enjoyed a most memorable bath—the only one in which my walls and ceiling were beautiful trees and sky.

One time we kids were especially energetic and bored, so we chased each other around the house. We literally ran around the outside of the entire house, which was something I never thought of doing in the projects. Neil would join us, and that would make it even funnier because as he chased us, we older kids caught up with him and passed him.

When I played alone, my toys were found in the great outdoors. I chased after the grasshoppers, crickets, and butterflies moving about in Grandma's flowerbeds and yard. I actually caught them with my bare hands, although as an adult I would prefer to use some type of gadget. I placed my catch in canning jars filled with grass, punched holes in the lids and learned that the butterflies only lived a few hours. I liked picking sour green apples off of Uncle Bernie's tree and looking at the colorful flower blossoms in Grandmother's front yard. Grandmother may have had other flowers in her garden, but I mostly remembered the bright yellow and orange giant marigolds that were almost as tall as I. They were there every summer so I learned to recognize them and their scent—a kind of spicy mint.

Usually at four o'clock in the afternoon, we ran up the dirt trail through the tall weeds to Aunt Bernice's trailer home. We'd see her car leading a cloud of dust as she entered the dirt road to her trailer and we knew that she was home from the Levi's factory. Her coming outside to sit in the shade of the trailer awning was our signal that it was okay to run up the path to greet her.

Most times, she delivered the ice pops we craved. She always shared her broad smile and sense of humor with us, revealing perfect teeth set off by dimples. As she sat fanning away the flies, she'd ask us all kinds of questions to amuse herself. I had trouble answering some of them, such as "What do ya'll do up there in New York?"

Once in a while, I got to take the "slop bucket," filled with kitchen scraps, up the path to the pigs owned by Uncle Bernie. Boy, did those pigs smell, but they held my attention! They ate whatever was in that slop bucket: rotten apples, bruised tomatoes, moldy vegetables, watermelon rinds, sour milk, stale bread, egg shells, and left-over food from dinner plates. Those pigs ate, greedily and voraciously, happily grunting and snorting as they chewed, drooled, swallowed and lifted their snouts for more. When the slop was consumed, I pulled up a certain weed growing along the fence and placed it by the nearest snout. It was quickly gobbled down as though it was a delicious morsel. I never asked an adult what kind of plant it was, but it smelled and looked like some kind of mint plant I discovered years later in my own yard. It was easy to recognize because it had fern-like leaves.

When it rained at Grandma's, time crawled to a snail's pace. There were only three TV stations and they went off at dusk. The radio stations were just as limited, and they only played two kinds of music—country and very country. When it thundered, Grandma made us turn off anything electric, which meant the lights, television and radio. We sat in silence to let "The Lord do His work." I thought that was very respectful. There were always family photos to look at. After looking through a box of pictures for the hundredth time, the best I could do sometimes was just go to bed early anticipating breakfast in the morning.

Summertime breakfasts could be huge events at Grandma Fields' house, especially on the morning after all of us relatives had arrived. All the women got busy in the kitchen preparing the biggest meal of the day, complete with scrambled eggs, fried green apples, hot buttery biscuits, bacon, sausage, orange juice, coffee and tea. We would all eagerly find a spot at the table and stuff ourselves until there was not even a scrap left for the pigs. It took half the morning to prepare and minutes to make it vanish.

The rest of the day dragged on after that yummy meal. As a service to Grandmother, I'd busied myself clearing the dining and living rooms of pesky houseflies before the evening meal, which was usually nothing fancy—just some kind of stew. I once killed over twenty houseflies singlehandedly with a simple fly swatter, hitting them any and everywhere—on the screen door, the window curtains, the kitchen table, the coffee table, the wall and the chairs. I leisurely gathered the dead flies one by one into a pile on the floor, scraped them all onto a paper plate, and then triumphantly carried them outside to throw them into the fiery flames of the wood pile.

No matter how much fun we had at Grandma's, it was always good to get back to hot water and indoor plumbing. By next summer, I would be ready to go again. I thought those leisurely days at Grandma's would never end. I never imagined her not being there and in looking back at Mom's people, I saw the seed of her strength.

After staying a week with Grandma Fields, we'd visit Daddy's people.

Chapter 7

Daddy's People

"The glory of young men is their strength."
Proverbs 20:29 (King James Version)

Like Grandma Fields, Grandma Alston also had a large family. She birthed and raised thirteen children. One should pause here just to ponder the implications of such a formidable task. The fact that it was typical for the American wife of that time to have many children does not belittle the feat; it is still a remarkable undertaking.

Dad did not share with me about his parents, youth, family life or any subject for that matter. The things I learned about his people were gathered from obituaries, other relatives and my own observations. That was not too much of a problem, for I liked to read, I've always been inquisitive and Grandmother Alston's heroic efforts produced a colorful bunch of uncles and aunts who were fascinating to observe.

Though they resembled one another in physical appearance, they possessed interesting and very diverse personalities. Dad and his siblings had light skin tones varying from cinnamon to cream, were all good-looking, equipped with deep, rich voices, round and broad noses, muscular and stocky bodies, and "good hair." (My understanding of "good hair" was the kind that remained attractive and manageable even after it got wet.) They towered above me in confidence, looks and assertiveness. I studied them from a quiet little corner hoping not to be noticed.

During festive family gatherings, I was able to get to know Dad's people a little. To my knowledge, all but two married and had children, so there was an endless flow of cousins, uncles and aunts throughout the house when we visited in the summer. Mealtimes were interesting events. We did not all sit down at one big table during family meals—it was just too impractical with that many people—but someone, usually the older sister, guarded the pots in the kitchen while you took what you could. Once during a backyard fish fry, I stood near the grill smelling a delicious aroma. The uncle cooking the fish pitied me and gave me a small portion, which I quickly gobbled. I continued to stand there desiring more, but somehow without any words spoken between us it was understood that what I got was all that I was going to get. I walked away wishing forever for more of that delicious fried fish.

My dad and his siblings were all born to Mrs. Nelonia Hazel McAdams Alston and Reverend William Clarence Alston. Grandpa Alston was born on February 12, 1895, the son of a short dark-skinned African-American man and a Caucasian midwife who traveled to neighboring homes to deliver babies. A daughter described my grandfather as a man "who was a loving father who loved to play and wrestle with his boys." She added that he was one of the founders of the Pilgrim's Rest Baptist Church and was a traveling preacher. He died at the age of fifty-six in 1951 from a cerebral hemorrhage.

According to her obituary, Dad's mother, Nelonia McAdams, was born on July 26, 1899, to Mr. and Mrs. L. D. McCallum in Alamance County, North Carolina. They were full-blooded Cherokee Indians. Her father abandoned her mother before she was born and stayed away for years. During that time, Grandmother Alston lost her mother, who died at the age of fifty-eight. When Great-Grandpa McCallum saw his daughter for the first time, she was married with many children. He stayed for a while and then disappeared again.

Grandma Alston grew up to be strong and productive. She earned wages working at home, where she could care for her children, by doing "the white people's laundry." She also made a living making beautiful quilts from scraps and dresses as a seamstress. Church was important to her for she spent many years as an active member of the African Methodist Episcopalian Church.

When we visited, I don't remember her speaking to me. I was one of many grandchildren she had running around the house. She always seemed busy and I can recall staring at her back as she sat at her sewing machine. I can still picture the two long, salt-and-pepper braids hanging down her back. I wished I had carefree hair like that. She gave Mom one of her beautiful patch quilts, which kept me warm at night. I felt privileged to have received something from her.

Perhaps Dad was attracted to Mom because she was beautiful, strong, and industrious like his mother. Maybe he wanted her to be the mother that he missed. I speculated because I was trying to understand the crazy forces that seem to drive my dad. I may never know.

* * *

Though I hardly knew her, I have much regard for my Grandmother Alston or for anyone who has borne and raised thirteen children, nine of whom were boys.

In March of 1917, at the age of eighteen, she gave birth to her firstborn, Charley William Saunders. World War I must have seemed far away for this new bride and mother living in rural North Carolina, as she looked upon her beautiful brown baby boy, who looked just like her.

Uncle Saunders became a member of his mother's church and later fell in love with the kind-hearted girl down the road named Gertrude. He married her at eighteen years of age in 1935. They had one child, Shirley, born in 1936. Three years later, the family of three joined the mass migration from the South, and resettled in Mount Vernon, New York. He served in World War II as a private first class in the United States Army, remained married to his wife for fifty-seven years, worked as a chauffeur for thirty years and lived in the same apartment for over twenty-five years.

Grandma Alston's second born arrived in 1919. She named her Evelyn. As the oldest girl, Aunt Evelyn was strictly no-nonsense. She left North Carolina, settled in Mount Vernon, married a Mr. Ricks and had a beautiful baby girl in 1938. This little girl, named Kay, was very successful in life, climbing up the social ladder from working class to upper middle class. Kay worked at Wellesley College in Massachusetts as a secretary in the personnel department. Her husband had a military career in the United States Air Force for over twenty years.

After moving to Mount Vernon, New York, Aunt Evelyn worked as a dress presser in a small shop. Sometimes Mom would ask her to watch me. During mealtime, she would make me eat my vegetables and not allow me to drink until all the food on the plate was gone. With her, there was absolutely no wastefulness concerning food. It was torture. She stood nearby, military-like, tall, muscular and intimidating, watching over me as I sat at the kitchen table. I didn't dare to argue with her and found a way to eat the food in front of me. When she retired, she moved back to live in North Carolina.

During the "roaring twenties," Grandma gave birth to five children. Child number three, James Matthew, came along in 1920. He picked up the nickname "Honey" along the way. Like his older brother, Uncle Honey had a full career before he retired, working at a local hospital as an orderly. He also enjoyed a long marriage to Aunt Juanita. He became an associate pastor of the Church of God and he stayed in North Carolina, near his mother, all of his life.

Uncle Honey won a special spot in my heart because one summer, he served as our host and made a meal for me that I will never forget. Rising up early, he prepared a generous breakfast of eggs, grits, sausage, biscuits, and orange juice and greeted Valerie and me with a warm and bubbly attitude when we walked into the kitchen. I was about eleven years old at the time and quite honored by his kindness, and I felt right at home. That was the first time a man prepared a meal for me. He was one of my favorite uncles.

Two years later in 1922, Auntie Ruth arrived as the fourth child. She was the epitome of cuteness, even as an adult, with long, black, wavy hair down her back and a wonderfully soothing southern drawl. She married and moved into a house on the same property as Grandma Alston's home, never leaving her mother's side. She had four children with Uncle Delmar, three boys and one girl, all handsome and beautiful.

High-spirited Aunt Lenora, number five, was born in 1924. She moved up to Mount Vernon following her two older brothers and older sister, Aunt Evelyn. We lived in the same apartment building for about six years. I remember her as a cool, confident woman who smiled often and who loved music, dancing, and laughter. When one of her favorite songs, "Sugar, Sugar," came on the radio, she got up and danced right there in the cramped kitchen, smiling from ear to ear, all by herself with complete ease, as I watched in awe. She amazed me because she was so comfortable in her own skin. She married and had three beautiful girls, who all did well in life, marrying, and working for AT&T and IBM until they retired. They all, including the mom, moved back to North Carolina after retirement.

In May of 1925, the sixth child, Clarence William (Bill), was born. Like his elder brother, he moved north to Mount Vernon at the age of seventeen and like his mom, joined an AME Zion church. He was very stable also. For twenty years, Uncle Bill found employment in a Yonkers hospital as a chef, and after marrying at twenty-one, remained joined to my aunt Mary in holy matrimony for forty-two years.

I always thought it was fantastic that two brothers (my father and Uncle Bill) married two sisters (my mom and Aunt Mary). Aunt Mary and Uncle Bill were my relatives twice over, both by marriage and by blood. They had no children together, but Aunt Mary made certain that I was always welcomed in their home, feeding me every time I visited, and I saw her on a regular basis because they lived only blocks away from us.

Uncle Bill always dressed dashingly, wearing the best in hats, suits and shoes, and driving fancy big Cadillacs. When I visited Aunt Mary, he would say a quick, disinterested "hi," and continued watching TV and smoking. As I grew older, I noticed that Uncle Bill was the life of the party, shocking and amusing people by the things he said.

In February of 1927, at twenty-eight years of age, Grandma Alston delivered her seventh child, George Richard. He left North Carolina, settled in Washington, D.C., fought in World War II, had four children by his first wife, Aunt Eunice, married a second time, and was a Baptist church member. He seemed good-natured whenever I encountered him, which was seldom.

The Great Depression during the early 1930s was hard on many American families. Times must have been especially hard for Grandma Alston as she produced a child every two years during this decade of scarcity. Aunt Evelyn was in her teens during the thirties and had lots of opportunity to hone her skills as rationing manager as she helped her mother feed the growing family.

In January of 1930, Grandma Alston, at thirty-one years of age, gave birth to her eighth, Joel Pittman. He became an elder at a Baptist church. He didn't stay in Burlington near his mom, nor follow his brothers to Mount Vernon. He and his wife, Florence, raised their two children in Newark, New Jersey. In my estimation, Uncle Joel was tall as a skyscraper, with bulging muscles. Like most of his brothers, he had little to say to me, but he displayed a mischievous grin as he looked down at me from that towering height. Then, menacingly, he proceeded to slowly pick me up and hold me suspended high above his shoulders with his arms fully outstretched. I was both intimidated and fascinated by his physical strength, but happy to have the attention. It was such a relief when he placed me safely back on my feet.

My father, the ninth child, was given a powerful ancient Greek name— Cornelius Alexander. (Grandma had endless creativity when it came to naming her children.) He was born in October 1932, right in the middle of the Depression years. As an adult, I asked him to talk about his family life. His answer was that they fought over chicken bones, had to eat chicken feet and made their own toys. He didn't seem comfortable going into any more detail, so I learned little from him.

In May of 1934, the tenth child, Margaret Lea, was born. She attended college, graduating from Winston-Salem State University and North Carolina A&T State University. She taught in the school system near her home. Aunt Margaret married Lawrence Smith, who attended two universities, served in the U.S. Army and was a United States Postal Service employee. They settled in Greensboro, North Carolina, where they raised their daughter.

The eleventh child, Uncle Nathanael, was born in 1936. When I met him in the 1960s, he was the only sibling who looked emaciated as though he was nearing death's door. He lived in Grandma's house and was always there when we visited. One summer, he was so sick that he coughed violently and constantly until the wee hours of the morning as he sat out on the porch. We kids were snuggled deep in our quilts on the floor of the front room adjacent to the porch, so I heard him all too well. I thought surely, by the sound of his hacking and gagging, that he would be found dead the next morning. Forty-two years later, at the time of this writing, he was doing just fine.

In the fall of 1938, her twelfth child, Thomas Earl, was born. He joined a Baptist church and worked at AT&T. He had a gift of music which was demonstrated when he taught himself to play the piano as a young boy. He worked with local church choirs, and some famous gospel groups and singers. He played dinner music at the Burlington Holiday Inn. At one family reunion in the 1960s, we all gathered around the piano and listened to him play Edwin Hawkins' hit gospel song, "Oh Happy Day." I was amazed. It sounded just like the recorded version. His obituary said that "he passed up many opportunities for nationwide fame because of his devotion to his beloved mother and his desire to be near her."

Grandma Alston delivered her last child, John Sterling, in 1941, when she was forty-two years old. I met him in my teens when he settled in Mt. Vernon. To me, he was the cutest of all the uncles. He had a charming boyish grin, an inquisitive mind, and was an independent thinker. I enjoyed his tendency to challenge me on an intellectual level. We had several conversations when he shared his understanding of the world with me, which was based on his studies of languages, religion and history. After hearing his rational arguments, my mind filled with doubts about Jesus. Yet, I could not deny my heart for years ago I experienced a life-changing encounter with the living Christ.

Thirty years later, Grandmother died a few weeks before her seventy-second birthday. At the time she died, she had twenty-one grandchildren and sixteen great-grandchildren. Once she died so did the major reason for visiting; thus the fascinating days of spending time with so many siblings and their families ended.

Grandma Alston flanked
by four of her children:
Uncle Bill, Dad,
Aunt Ruth, and
Uncle Honey.

The 13 siblings in the late
1970's: Left to right:
Dad, Uncle George (kneeling).
Middle row: Uncle Saunders,
Auntie Ruth, Aunt Evelyn,
Aunt Lenora, Uncle Thomas
and Aunt Margaret.
Back Row: Uncle Joel,
Uncle John, Uncle Nay and Uncle Honey.
(courtesy of Art John)

* * *

Sixteen years after Grandma Alston's death, the grim reaper began his ugly work and took away over half of Grandmother Alston's children almost as rapidly as they had come into the world. It lingered long enough to claim the lives of seven Alston children in a period of ten years.

In August of 1987, Uncle George died at age sixty, after a long illness.

The following year, in February 1988, I was saddened when I heard that the family buried my strong and powerful uncle Joel, who died after a long illness at the age of fifty-eight. Another funeral was planned that summer, when in the heat of July my cool uncle Bill, who didn't visit doctors but smoked regularly, dropped to the ground from cardiac arrest while he wiped the morning dew off his Cadillac. He was sixty-three years old and was visiting the family in North Carolina, with plans to buy a home and retire there.

The family had a rest from funerals for four years. Then in 1992, Uncle Saunders died of lung cancer at seventy-five years of age. The following year, and nine years after her husband's death, Aunt Margaret died of cancer at age fifty-eight. She had been retired from the school system for three years.

Two years later, the family buried another sibling, in February 1994. Our gifted musician, Uncle Thomas, died at fifty-six years of age, leaving behind a will to the estate that caused division. About fifteen relatives, including two living brothers (Dad was one), a sister and several children of five deceased siblings, sued the estate and won. My dad's portion of the settlement was $5,000, which he received in 2000.

1997 began with the death of Uncle Honey in the middle of a snowy January. He was seventy-seven years old. Thus, in a relatively short time span, six sons and one daughter were taken away. I was afraid at one point that the funerals would not stop until all of my uncles and aunts were gone, but thankfully, the rapid succession of burials ceased, but by the time things quieted down, the glory of the Alston clan had dimmed.

Only two brothers and three sisters were alive at the time when Dad was so desperately ill. I am sure that, like me, they had good reasons for not being at Dad's side. All of his older brothers were gone. Furthermore, Daddy probably distanced himself even more from his family members by involving himself in the lawsuit over the estate. Once I realized that Dad had no close friends or relatives, it left me feeling the weight of his alienation.

I did have a cousin, Dad's niece, who lived nearby in Baltimore. She helped tremendously by accompanying Neil on his visits to see Dad in the hospital. She spent hours with me over the phone. Her advice and concern were very comforting.

How different it would have been if Daddy had a loving wife to help him during his illnesses. Maybe, if that were the case, he would not be struggling for his life right now at the not-so-old age of sixty-eight. Yet, Daddy did have a good wife. Why did he let her go?

Chapter 8

Glasses, Hair and Fights

"What causes fights and quarrels among you? Aren't they caused by the selfish desires that fight to control you?"
James 4:1 (GOD'S WORD)

It was 1968 and all of the members of my family were strong and full of promise. As the days of summer began to shorten and the leaves turned brilliant shades of yellow, orange and red, I entered fourth grade. The teacher noticed my squinting to see the writing on the chalkboard, so she alerted the school nurse, who alerted my mom, who promptly took me to an optician. I was diagnosed with myopia or nearsightedness, and Mom made sure that I received my first pair of glasses.

I was amazed at how defined the world looked through my new glasses. People's faces across the street were no longer blurry and the leaves on the trees were separate and distinct little entities. I could read the signs in the store windows and on the billboards as Mom drove me around in the car. I wore my thick, large-framed glasses all the time after I saw the difference they made, even if Keith laughed at me.

Keith was a peer, a son of my mom's friend who lived in one of the apartment towers. He took one look at me as I stood in the parking lot of our apartment building, pointed in my direction, and then threw his head back laughing hilariously. I wanted him to stop and told him so. He didn't, but continued laughing his guts out, so I chased him around the parking lot until he ran out of sight.

As a pre-teen, I was subjected to all kinds of negative comments about my appearance by peers. I grew so discouraged from the names and mean words that many times when I was alone in my room, I cried. I could hear the ugly words in my head. "Your ears are so small! You got little monkey ears! Nappy head!! Skinny legs! Pug nose! Ugly! Chicken legs! Four-eyes!" Believing the words to be true, I did not even try to defend myself but quietly and passively accepted the abuse. I sank further into depression.

Mom did her best to make sure I didn't look too scary. She paid for me to have my hair washed and pressed every two weeks. Miss B., the hairdresser, had a shop in the basement of her home, a few blocks away from our apartment building. She washed, dried, pressed and curled my hair for ten dollars. Miss B. never said anything, but she treated my hair as though it was horrendous. She attacked it with as much heat as she could. After shampooing it, she'd sprinkle a black liquid that stank like tar (or oil from some guy's car repair shop) over my hair and then tugged at the tangles with a merciless comb as I sat under the nozzle of a blistering hot blow-dryer. The heavy iron pressing comb was heated to just below hair-scorching temperature, and with it she pressed my hair until it was bone straight and shiny. Next, she used super-hot curling irons to form tight curls. She was very skilled and did all this within an hour, but I walked out of there every time with tight, unnatural, greasy curls. She did not apply a protective hair conditioner on my hair or clip the ends, so for a long time my hair was dry, stringy and damaged. Miss B. wasn't the only beautician who treated my hair as though it was "bad hair." The first hairdresser to permanently relax my hair chose a super-strength lye formula which was too strong—it burned my scalp and left oozing sores that turned into scabs. Hence, during my youth, my hair never grew to any length because of continual breakage. If I wanted the feel of long hair, I would throw a towel over my head and dance around the room shaking my head as the towel flipped around my face like gorgeous locks.

Sometime during my twenties, I broke down and complained to God, "Why did You give me such dreadful hair—nothing can be done with it!" I wanted to just fall out and cry, but I knew that would be a waste of time. I stopped accusing God and asked for wisdom and over time saw results. As my hair improved, I realized that God did not give me damaged and brittle hair, but mistreatment did. After that "heavy revy," I read Naomi Sims' book, *All About Hair Care For the Black Woman*, over and over again and learned how to handle it myself. I am at peace with my hair now and am very thankful to still have some after all it's gone through.

With so many self-esteem issues, I hated my life. I didn't feel that I belonged on the earth and I often yearned to go to heaven where I knew I'd be loved. I'd say to God, "You can take me home now." I thought about jumping out of our seventh-floor window, but was too afraid of all the pain and attention it might cause. When I attended a funeral, I was envious of the person in the box and would say, "Lord, how about me?"

Since I had good health and always woke up the next morning, I figured that the Lord wanted me to live. His silence was my answer. He didn't want me in Heaven yet. I felt worse. Even God didn't want me. I was an absolute reject! I'd cry some more.

The Lord wonderfully took what was evil in my life and turned it around for my good. All of my misery pushed me closer to Him as I found great satisfaction and comfort in reading the Bible and hanging around God's people at church. His teachings, whether they were in word or song, became air, water and bread to me.

* * *

School was starting up again soon and Mom wanted to take us to get new clothes and shoes. I heard her and Dad talking in the kitchen. She was trying to get money again. I wished that she would not risk asking him. *Just leave him alone, Mom,* I thought to myself

"The children need school clothes, Cornelius! School starts next week and they have nothing to wear!

"They got clothes last year!"

"But they have outgrown those clothes already! They can't fit in last year's clothes, they need new ones!"

"I got no money for clothes! Patch them up, stretch them out! They should use what they got!"

"I'm not letting my kids go to school looking raggedy, with clothes that don't fit, and that are all worn out, Cornelius! My children are not going to school looking like they have no mother at home!"

Mom had pride. She wanted her children to look their best. Daddy didn't worry about stuff like that. If he grew up without new clothes every season, so could we. It was not a necessity in his thinking.

"Well, maybe if I get lucky, they'll have new clothes."

"Lucky?!! Cornelius, I know you just got paid, where is all that money? The children cannot go to school in rags! I have to buy the groceries and Felicia's and Neil's glasses, so the least you can do is to help with the clothes and shoes!"

"Don't worry about my money. I pay the rent! NOW STOP BOTHERING ME AND SHUT UP OR I WILL SHUT YOU UP!"

"The rent! Is that all you're going to help with when there are so many other…"

Mom couldn't continue because Dad cut in.

"YOU KEEP NAGGING ME, WOMAN…SHUT UP, DOGGONIT, OR I'LL MAKE YOU!

He was bursting with anger and his eyes were starting to pop out. He started after Mom, grabbed a hard object and hurled it in her direction. Mom dodged out of the way as it crashed to the floor. I was frozen with fear in the adjacent room as I heard Daddy raucously exit out the door.

Somehow, Mom brought us new clothes for school. I got three new outfits and a new pair of shoes and I felt ready for that first day of school. Through her sheer hard work and determination, she always managed to earn the money to take care of our physical needs, and that was a demanding job with three children.

She had married a man who had other priorities besides taking care of his wife and children, but she did not let him break her strong spirit. After working all night in the hospital, she was up and busy working when I got home from school. My mother could burn the rope at both ends. She could rise up early and go to bed late at night and still be perky and energetic throughout the day as she did several tasks at once. When I arrived home from school, I often found her watching the sizzling romances of soap operas, but only as she continued to do her chores such as ironing clothes. She was married, but living more like a single parent. From my vantage point today, I can see how Dad began to lose Mom's devotion. I don't know if she ever got enough sleep during those years.

* * *

She made such a burning impression that I can still visualize, my fifth-grade teacher. Miss S. always wore a red jumper with a white blouse. The aroma of crisp, smoked bacon or perhaps chewing tobacco drifted across the room as she marched to the front of the class, looking straight ahead, with the chin up. Her military demeanor made several of us kids emit muted giggles.

I hung out with a female classmate I admired, who I'll call Perky. She was a slender dark-brown-skinned girl who wore cat-eye glasses and pulled her hard-pressed hair back into a ponytail, leaving a curled bang over her forehead. She possessed a great smile, decorated with dimples, set nicely in her heart-shaped face. I wanted to be like her because she was smart, perky and confident and because she had enough hair to fit into a ponytail. She reminded me of an upcoming royal professional carrying herself with perfect poise. Then there was a tall, dark-chocolate, handsome boy who I adored who was a true Black Beauty. I'll call him Black Beauty. He had a milk-chocolate friend, who was not as tall, who I think had eyes for me, but I was only interested in Black Beauty. However Black Beauty liked Perky, who had the pep in her step and those regal high cheekbones. I don't recall who Perky liked.

That winter, we girls wore the popular, multi-colored wool stocking caps. Each colorful knit cap was made with a long tail with a pompom on the end which was perfect for grabbing and snatching. As we walked home from school, the boys chased us to pull off our caps, then bombarded us with snowballs. I was an excellent runner, so I only got caught once.

I lost my glasses. I listened as Mom embarked on another attempt to get money out of Dad. She was a fighter. Her father was a provider and she was not accustomed to being neglected. I would have given up long ago, but she was determined to remind Dad about his duties as a father. I braced for another unnerving scene.

"The child needs glasses, Cornelius," Mom pleaded.

"She got glasses. She just got a pair last year!" Daddy argued.

"She lost that pair, and besides her prescription has changed! She has to have a new pair!"

"I am sick and tired of buying her glasses!" Dad retorted.

"I brought the pair last year, Cornelius!" Mom corrected.

"Well, good! You buy them then…and stop bothering me! I pay the rent! I'm not giving you no money for glasses that she just throws away. If she lost them, she don't need to have 'em."

I was hurt by what I heard. It was no use for Mom to try to convince Dad. He didn't need glasses; his vision was fine. If it was up to him I would have to walk about with poor vision and maybe even go blind. It was frightening to think of what would happen to me if I could not see well enough to handle schoolwork, which was a main source of my self-esteem. I cringed at the thought of shrinking into oblivion, locked away in an institution because I could not take care of myself when I was grown. What saddened me more was the idea that my dad would stand by and watch my life ebb away as though it was no concern of his. My self-esteem dropped down to a near zero.

Mom made sure I had new glasses as she secretly prayed for God to take Dad far away from her.

Daddy with Neil who is two years old.

Me, aged 10.

Valerie, 4 years, and me,
2 years, about to go for
a Sunday's ride.

Mom and Dad
on their wedding day (1957)

My parents as a young couple. (circa 1957)

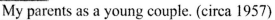

* * *

At the end of fifth grade, when we were all about age ten or eleven years old, Black Beauty, Milk Chocolate, some other girl and I went into the basement of my projects building. To me, the damp and dark basement's only purpose was to serve as an alternate route outdoors, and I always ran through it quickly, but today I was with Black Beauty. The building janitor was not around to drive away us loitering kids. We could tell since the door to the incinerator room was secured with a padlock. The coast being clear, Black Beauty pulled out a cigarette, lit it, put it to his lips, inhaled and passed it around. I watched, thinking, *Why is this gorgeous boy wanting to do something that is not healthy for that beautiful body of his!* He inhaled deeply and passed the cigarette to me. I forced myself to take it. I did it for him. I raised it to my mouth and let it touch my bottom lip, then inhaled ever so weakly. The little trace of smoke that I think entered my airway caused a fit of coughing and hacking. I must have looked like an idiot as I broke away from the circle to concentrate on effective coughing.

I forgot about pleasing Black Beauty as my mind filled up with logic and old-fashioned common sense. I heeded. I was the worst candidate for becoming a smoker. When adults used cigarettes around me, the second-hand smoke irritated me to no end and all I could think about was getting away to fresh air. Even sometimes fresh air was an irritant to my sensitive mucous membranes. After hours of playing outside in the wonderful month of May, breathing in the invigorating spring air, I'd have to rush inside the building, run up the six flights, dash into our apartment, and spend a few hours inside to find relief. I furiously rubbed my itching, watery red eyes until they swelled up like balloons and could not be opened. My nose was on the rampage also, pouring out streams of clear liquid as I engaged in a fit of continuous sneezing, using up half a box of tissues. I was diagnosed with hay fever. It was obvious that with such a sensitive head on my shoulders, I would never become a cigarette smoker without a bitter battle against my body's natural defense reflexes, and I was not much of a fighter.

After failing miserably at the secret-smokers club initiation, I moved on to summer fun without Black Beauty in my life. I decided to set up a Kool-Aid stand on one hot summer day in July. Mom let me borrow her things: a chair, a small folding table, a pitcher for the iced red Kool-Aid and a bag of five-ounce paper cups. I strategically placed my stand outside the building entrance, in the path of tired mothers walking home in the hot sun from the business district or from their stand-up jobs, their arms burdened with shopping bags and groceries. My sign "Cold Kool-Aid—Five Cents" caught their eye like a mirage in the desert. As the weary travelers approached, they had little choice but to rest and purchase. I sold forty cups of Kool-Aid for five cents, took the two dollars I made and sponsored a picnic for a few of my friends. The menu included penny candy, two-cent cookies, five-cent ice pops and ten-cent potato chips. I spread the menu items over a blanket on the grass and we sat down to feast. If he had known, maybe Daddy would have been proud of my entrepreneurship.

Later that summer, Mom took us to Grandma Fields' house, on the only form of transportation she could afford for long-distance travel—the Greyhound bus. I was old enough to sit alone and I especially remember that trip because of a Gideon New Testament that I had. I read the first Gospel and couldn't stop. I was captivated. I soaked up page after page of wonderful news about Jesus until I read all four Gospels of Matthew, Mark, Luke and John. During that trip, I was astounded at what I learned about Jesus. He was so wonderful, so perfect, so all-knowing and powerful, yet He helped the least of people, those who were despised and rejected: the short tax collector, the ten lepers, the man born blind, the woman who lost her youthful glow to a bleeding problem, the cripple, the cheating wife, the man who lived in the graveyard mutilating himself, and the thief on the cross, just to name a few.

God's Word spoke directly to me. It was filled with wonderful words I craved to hear. *"I am the way, the truth and the life…" (John 14:6). "I am the bread of life…he that cometh to me shall never hunger and he that believeth on me shall never thirst." (John 6:35). "I am the light of the world; he that followeth me shall not walk in darkness, but shall have the light of life"(John 8:12). "But whosoever drinketh of the water that I shall give him shall never thirst; but the water that I shall give him shall be in him a well of water springing up into everlasting life" (John 4:14). "But seek ye first the kingdom of God, and his righteousness; and all these things shall be added unto you" (Matthew 6:33). "…Suffer little children, and forbid them not, to come unto me: for of such is the kingdom of heaven" (Matthew 19:14).* The words filled my hungry soul and began a work deep within me. *"But the very hairs of your head are all numbered. Fear ye not therefore, ye are of more value than many sparrows" (Matthew 10:30-31).*

I realized more than ever that God wanted and loved me—a skinny, "four-eyed" little African American girl with short hair living in the projects, without her daddy's love. His Word filled me with hope.

After that bus ride, I was hooked. Whenever I felt depressed, which was almost every day, I'd read the Bible. I read His Word regularly for as I ingested its meaning, I was constantly reminded that I was in God's hands, that He loved me and that He had a plan for my life. I believed every word.

Chapter 9

A Step Down

"Like a clay pot covered with cheap silver, so is smooth talk that covers up an evil heart."
Proverbs 26:23 (GOD'S WORD)

In our own way, we loved each other, but there was never a whole lot of communication in our family. During the summer of 1970, when I was eleven years old, there was a big change in our lives. We were moving and I had no idea that this huge event was coming or why. I was told to pack up one day and shortly afterwards we moved from my familiar paradise to a gloomier place six blocks away. We probably needed to move into a three-bedroom apartment so that Neil could have his own room. After all, he was six and too old to continue sharing a bedroom with Mom and Dad. There may have been other reasons for moving, but regardless of the reasons, I quickly adapted and followed my family.

Our new home was in an apartment building that looked a hundred years old. Compared to the Levister Towers, it was an old shrimp of a building with only four levels, creaky wooden stairways and no elevator! We were all young and healthy, so the top fourth-floor apartment suited us just fine. On one side of the building was a rusting, iron fire-escape leading down to a dirty, dismal alley. In the front, our building was connected to a twin building by a façade. This other building housed mainly Hispanic tenants. Ours was home to a mixture of white, African-American and Hispanic families.

We were now on a street comprised of a potpourri of old colonials, Victorians, and a few other low-rise apartment buildings like ours. It was a good thing that I was maturing, for here on this block there really were no good places to run and play. The new play area was in the hallway or out on the sidewalk along a busy, one-way street cluttered with parked cars. A neglected playground and a vacant lot were at the other end of the block. The remaining few pieces of playground equipment were rusty and broken. The adjacent vacant lot filled with rocks, weeds, broken glass and litter, was only good for letting Frisky loose to run. She was the dog (part German Shepherd, part Collie, part something other) Mom got for Neil that quickly became my dog because I took care of her.

Frisky and I.

Though this move was a step down into a rougher neighborhood, it quickly became home. There were two beautiful trees in front of the building and two decorative, waist-high, flat-top concrete columns that were good places to sit, on either side of the steps leading to the front door. I sat out on one of those half-pillars many summer nights, enjoying conversations with the other tenants, including relatives since Aunt Lenora, Dad's sister, lived on the third floor and Aunt Mary and Uncle Bill lived in the apartment building across the street.

FELICIA JOHNSON

Valerie and I squeezed our things into a bedroom so tiny that a bunk bed was the only option. We took turns on who slept on the more desirable lower bunk. We became more like sisters rooming in that tiny space, sharing clothes, watching the same television shows and listening to the same music although we still had very different social circles. We enjoyed listening to Billy Preston's instrumental "Outta Space" and played it over and over again on a record player that was placed on top of a bureau in a corner of the room. I learned that my sister was very generous. If I asked, Valerie would let me borrow her more fashionable clothes and earrings.

Neil had his own room and kept it very neat. Mom made sure the "super," or maintenance man, who happened to be Dad, allowed her to get a dog for Neil. Dad sought out the position of building superintendent because it offered very low rent in exchange. He also installed a washing machine for her beside the sink in the kitchen. After washing the clothes, we hung our clothes out to dry on a clothesline overlooking the alleyway that stretched from our living room window to a window in the adjacent building. When clothes fell off the line down into the alley, I had to go around the building into that eerie, dirty place to retrieve them. Fearing rats, dogs and derelicts, I was always relieved to come back out alive.

As Mom and Dad's union unraveled, so did my last glimmer of hope that Dad would be a father to me. I felt very excited one summer evening when he invited me to go to work with him the next day. He was actually asking me to spend time with him! This was a wonderful thing to me for it meant that I was not repulsive to him. Maybe it was because I was now twelve and no longer an annoying little kid. I didn't know the reason, but it felt good that he asked me to be a part of his world for a day.

The next morning, at 5:30 a.m., I rushed out of bed to leave with Dad. I didn't have time to eat breakfast and didn't think to pack a lunch. We were merging onto the highway before sunrise on our way to Long Island. We rode silently, but I sat in that car filled with happy expectations. I was going to learn about my dad and I was no longer someone of whom he was ashamed.

When we arrived, I followed him into the building. His place of work was a brick building with few windows. Inside, it looked like a warehouse. There was a huge open area filled with long tables covered with wires, electronic devices and small hand tools. I was a bit disappointed when Dad didn't talk to me or explain anything. He motioned for me to sit at a table out of view from

74

his work area. He didn't introduce me to anyone. As I settled down at the table, I realized that I was on my own again. I did not want to bother Dad by needing attention. Wishing I had brought a book, I looked for something to do. There were some wires, a few washers and bolts and a pair of pliers lying on the table in front of me. To pass the time, I started twisting some of the wires into shapes with the pliers.

As noon approached, my stomach started twisting like the wires in my fingers. I was feeling hunger pangs which I never experienced under Mom's care. I knew it would annoy Daddy if I told him about my problem. My heart sank. I wondered why I even allowed myself to get into this predicament. I should have packed a lunch. I was sorry that I had entrusted myself to his care. I should have known better. I started feeling a slight pounding in my head, as my stomach cramped. Then I felt nauseous and weak.

I tried to take my mind off the hunger pains by forcing myself to daydream. I rested my head on my folded arms and closed my eyes. I pictured a green meadow with soft grass and pretty little flowers. I was running at first, but then, no, it was more like stumbling…to a little house. Inside the house was a kitchen table…covered with a pretty tablecloth. Then, my mind turned against me. Spread across the table, I saw Grandma Fields' yummy breakfasts of scrambled eggs, fried apples, hot biscuits, sausage, and milk. I tried to shake the image but it stuck in my pounding head. My stomach cramped. I felt faint and could take it no longer.

I decided that I just had to have something to eat. I noticed a food bar near the entrance. The only problem was…I had no money. I would just have to be bold, bear the indignation and do what I hated doing most…ask Dad for money. I really did not want to bother him; I didn't like being annoying. However, I didn't really have a choice. Either I aggravated him by asking for money or upset him by passing out at his job. I walked over to where he was sitting.

"Dad, I'm very hungry. I don't have any money." I braced myself.

"What!" He looked irritated.

"I need some money to buy something to eat, please?"

I hardly looked him in the eye.

He looked totally disgusted as though I really needed to get my act together. Maybe he assumed that Mom had given me some money. Whatever the case, he impatiently dug into his pocket and tossed some money on the table between us.

It was enough to buy a plain breakfast sandwich consisting of a fried egg between two pieces of dry toast. I wanted something to drink, like orange juice, but didn't bother Daddy again. I'd look around for a water fountain later. I never forgot how delicious that sandwich tasted. I ate it and was revived. I had nothing else to eat until we got home after 6:00 that evening. We rode home in silence. I never wanted to burden him again.

If Dad had spoken with me on the way home that evening, he might have described how he went many days as a child suffering from hunger pains. Maybe he would have explained how he had to fight and fend for survival amongst all those siblings. Getting his basic needs met must have been hard at times. I'm sure he had loads of stories to tell me, having twelve siblings and all, but he didn't share his life experiences and I still suffer that loss.

Dad was tough and independent, like he is now; suffering alone in that hospital and needing no one at his side, not even a daughter who wanted to help. I am sure he had reasons for telling me to wait until he was better. Maybe he was embarrassed that he was so helpless or maybe he didn't have the energy to deal with his child. Whatever his reason, I felt it best if I honored it. I suppose it was easier for both of us to continue to act like strangers.

My big and strong dad was an illusion. When his brothers or sisters confronted him about not doing enough for his family, he denied it. He insisted that he was a good father who provided for us and he continued to act as though all was well. I never understood his thinking. Perhaps he was comparing himself to someone far worse.

When reading the Bible one day, I came across a verse in Proverbs chapter 23 that compared a person who used smooth words to cover up his stony heart to a clay pot painted with cheap silver and I sadly thought of my daddy. He was my father who appeared promising on the surface, ornamented with strength, talents, intelligence and potential, but when actually called upon to deliver, offered disappointment and emptiness.

In describing my relationship with Dad, I have borrowed a phrase from this verse. I know that we are all formed from clay, but what we each strive to contribute to our world is something much more wonderful and lasting. Most of us desire to impart to our children gifts of solid beauty and value. It doesn't always work out that way. In my case, what I have received from my father can best be described as an empty pot of "silver-coated clay."

After spending a day with Daddy, it depressed me to look at the pot. I put it out of my mind, in a dark corner under the bed, and went on with my life.

Chapter 10

Hooked on Clay

"One who is full despises honey, but to one who is hungry, even bitter food tastes sweet."
Proverbs 27:7 (GOD'S WORD)

After we moved, Mom continued attending the same church and I followed right behind her. Instead of one block away, the church was now six blocks away and it made for a pleasant, but fast walk. I always walked quickly and purposeful through the streets of Mount Vernon in order to send out a clear message that I was not looking for a man, drugs or a fight. Mom attended the main service at eleven o'clock, but I still liked to go also to the 9:30 a.m. Sunday school.

The Sunday school service was meant especially for the young people. We teens sat in age-appropriate groups scattered throughout the sanctuary. A volunteer church mother, trying hard to remain patient, would strive to keep us on track with the lesson, having us read aloud and answer the application questions from quarterly lesson booklets. There were no snacks, DVD's, MP3's, PSP's, video games, ping pong tables, movies, slide shows, flannel graph or even puppets. It was just the teacher, the kids, the pews and the booklets. I was an oddball because I loved sitting around reading and discussing God's Word. We never went into enough detail for me. Needless to say, I didn't have too many friends.

I began the New Year of 1972 walking to Sunday school in the rain. On the way home, I stopped at a candy store and brought two comic books, *Love and Romance* and *Teen-Age Love*. As a thirteen-year-old with an intense curiosity of romantic love, I purchased lots of comic books that year. I watched many movies about love and read lots of paperback romance stories. One of my favorites was a thin paperback picture book I purchased entitled, *I Was A Lonely Teenager*. In that story, the rejected, lonely girl finally found love. It was very encouraging.

As the days grew warmer and the few trees along our sidewalk sprouted little flowers, a new family moved into the building. Suddenly, life was full of suspense and excitement. It seemed that every time Valerie and I ascended the creaky stairway something strange and exhilarating happened. The door of the apartment near the top landing would crack open just a bit, enough to expose an eye, and a gorgeous one at that. It belonged to a dark, handsome young man around Valerie's age. When we looked in his direction, he'd quickly close the door.

Valerie and I could not wait to meet the rest of him. One afternoon Neil, who was eight years old, and a boy my age were out in the hall playing a little one-on-one basketball game with a toy net and a foam ball. They were playing in front of the door belonging to the spy. Overcome with curiosity, Valerie and I decided that this was our chance to meet the new neighbors. After all, we had a perfectly good reason to loiter in the hallway; our little brother was out there. We quietly sat down on the staircase near our door. We pretended to mind our own business as we listened for every word. In addition to the noise of the boys' playing, we soon heard heavy footsteps ascending the staircase below us. A grumpy resident, who lived alone, was coming home. Before he entered his apartment which was right next to that of the new neighbors, he scolded Neil and his friend.

"Get away from my door! Find someplace else to play your game! This ain't no d**m basketball court!"

Neil and his friend walked over to continue their game directly in front of where we sat. Now, we had front-row seats! Valerie, being the more sociable one, broke the ice by telling silly jokes and laughing at any and everything. The handsome spy, who was tall and a shorter guy, soon entered the hallway. Now there were three handsome teenage boys all directing their undivided attention upon us! The taller one sat on the floor, over next to the watchman's door, while the shorter one leaned on the railing, peeking down at me as I giggled. I glanced back at him and he immediately turned his face away. He did not impress me, anyway. He was not my type—much too shy and insecure. Mom called us in and that ended our first encounter.

Later that night, the tallest guy was out in the hall again. When Valerie and I heard his footsteps and whistling through the walls, our hormones drove us right back out into the hall. He said it was too hot in his place for his allergies. We agreed that the hallway was definitely the place to be.

I learned that evening that the basketball player was my age and he was the one who interested me. I'll call him Bounce. He was lean, muscular and a beautiful brown. He had a round face with large, expressive eyes and long eyelashes. His body was well proportioned and agile. His hair was cut in a short natural. I could see that his ears stuck out from his head just enough to be adorable. His most alluring quality to me was that he seemed very comfortable in his skin. He glanced at me as he played basketball. Over the course of the summer he won my heart.

One morning in June, after walking Frisky, I sat on the building's front steps enjoying the morning air and warmth of the sun. I heard someone bounding down the stairs skipping two or three steps at a time. It was Bounce, who stepped lively and rhythmically down the hallway to the front entrance and sat beside me, smelling fresh and clean and wearing blue jeans with a bright white T-shirt. He was just so smooth and confident, I could hardly look at him in the eye, I was so nervous. He fingered the back of my neck with soft, warm fingers and spoke enticing words.

"Where have you been all my life?" was the line this thirteen-year-old used to sweep me off my feet.

I couldn't answer. I sat there staring at the dog leash, soaking up his every word and wanting to hear more!

Then he took my breath away.

"I'm going to marry you."

My heart leaped. I didn't answer him, but thought to myself, *Yes, yes. Finally someone to love me and yes, I will marry you!* I put his words in a special, anti-erase memory vault in my heart. He got up when his buddies arrived and together they walked off, he with rhythm and bounce in his step, picking out his hair with a wide-tooth Afro pick. I floated off with dreamy thoughts of love.

The next time I saw Bounce it was from Mom's bedroom window a few evenings later. He was outside with shorts on revealing legs that were beautiful and well-defined. He was playing with a younger boy. I ran down the three flights of stairs and sat inside the building foyer with Frisky, and soon developed enough nerve to go outside to where he was. He was playing with a stick by then and when he saw me he teased saying that the stick looked like one of my legs. I didn't respond to him, but when no one was paying me any attention, I went back up to the apartment, put on pair of pants and returned outside.

"Why did you change?" he asked annoyingly as he pushed me off the pillar seat back into a small area of dirt meant for gardening that was surrounded by a black iron fence. Though I tried to act tough, I enjoyed every minute of his bantering.

"Let me out of here," I said with a smile.

"No, you're in jail," he replied.

He eventually backed away so that I could climb back into a sitting position on the half pillar. Then he proceeded to entertain me with songs and jokes, while I laughed and adored him, wishing that I could have him around forever.

A few days later, my sister Valerie, Bounce, another guy and I hung out in the building hallway with a tenant girl who I'll call Slender. She was a teenager, a little older than Valerie. She wore a short Afro that still allowed her to look attractive and feminine and was tall, lanky and dark skinned. She smoked and was really comfortable around guys, and I admired the ease with which she carried herself.

As we sat on the steps of the stairway, I had them all sign my autograph book. Bounce wrote in it, in sloppy handwriting, "I love you…" When everyone teased him about what he had written, he reacted in a way that hurt me deeply.

"She's ugly!" he complained.

"Why you calling her ugly?" Slender asked in my defense.

"That's what she is," he answered.

My sister then spoke up.

"Well, how come you wrote this?" she demanded.

"I had my eyes closed," he replied.

I sat on higher steps to get away from the group. I felt as though I was going to cry. I felt cursed by my appearance. The group's attention turned to something else and after a few minutes, I went into the apartment.

While they continued on in lively chatter, I decided to get ready for bed by fixing my hair for the night. In order to maintain a head of curls for the each day, I regularly rolled my hair into foam curlers and slept in them all night. As I was rolling a section of hair, I looked at myself in my bedroom mirror and saw that I didn't look so bad, so I took out the roller and mustered the courage to go into the kitchen to peek at the group through the screen door. Bounce immediately came over and I retreated back into the house. He followed me in. I told him to get out. He would not, so I grabbed a broom and raised it, threatening to crack him over the head with it. He stood there with a look of amusement on his face.

I smiled.

He laughed and then said, "I want a kiss."

I pushed him out, shut the door and went back into my room. Feeling vindicated, I went to bed for the night.

He spent enough time with me that summer to make me crave his company even more. I was his perfect audience, his biggest fan, hooked by his words of affection, ability to make me laugh and the love songs he sang to me. I reasoned that he was only being honest when he sometimes called me derogatory names, so I overlooked that and hung on.

By the end of the summer, I wasn't so special to him anymore. I had to listen to him brag.

"I have so many girls, Felicia, did you know that? I have Janna, Carla— some girl I met playing basketball—and you!" he said as he looked me in the eye and counted the names on his fingers.

"Not me!" I replied, feeling jealous and disappointed.

"You better be!" he calmly warned.

It was about eight o'clock on a dusky, chilly night. The cooler weather marked a change in our relationship. Bounce was holding his wallet for some reason. I grabbed it and searched it for any bits of information I could find out about this secretive guy who I felt was slipping away from me.

"Don't look at the paper with my nickname on it," he said, watching me closely.

There was no such paper. I found two pictures of his family members. There was also an identification card and a piece of paper with his name and address. For a fleeting moment, looking through his wallet made me feel closer to him.

I had to accept his liking other girls. I could not do a thing about that. In his presence, I acted indifferent so that he would not see my sadness. With my mind I understood that it was only natural that he should lose interest in me and go after prettier, flashier girls. That reasoning did not help with the pain in my heart. To deal with it, I tried my old defense strategy of creating a distance between us. I did my best to pretend he didn't exist.

A few weeks went by of not seeing him. One evening in September, I was out walking Frisky. When I came back to the building, Bounce was outside. I was glad to see him and hoped that my looks would be acceptable to him. I had tried to fix my hair better. Combing it back with a part down the middle was the best I could do that day. He immediately started making comments.

"Sneakers starting to talk…hair looks Indian…whose coat?" he remarked as he sized me up and down.

I didn't answer much. I simply did not have the confidence, skills or money to try to look glamorous. We sat down on the steps in the building foyer. He flipped his fingers around in my hair and felt my neck. I rubbed my dog Frisky's coat to avoid looking at him. Two other guys (a tall one and a shorter one) soon joined us so I ended up with the three guys alone in the foyer as the darkness fell. The tallest guy had something sinister on his mind because as he was standing in front of me, he started swaying side to side as he sung a made up tune.

"I want some *u-s-s-y*," he sang several times over.

He was starting to annoy me. I wanted to spend time alone with Bounce and wished the other two would just disappear or at least continue to where they needed to be. They were ruining my time with Bounce.

"Do you know what *r-a-i-p* spells?" the older guy blurted out suddenly.

"No," I responded tersely. I knew what he was trying to spell but I didn't appreciate the subject and I certainly did not want to talk with him about it.

"It stands for rape!" he smirked, looking very devilish.

My "teacher instinct" kicked in. I had to help this guy out so that he would not embarrass himself later.

"*Rape* is spelled *r-a-p-e* not *r-a-i-p*," I corrected, hoping he'd go home and do some homework.

"She's right," the shorter one said.

The taller one kicked the shorter one into a filthy corner.

"I told you she was smart," Bounce chimed in, as he played in my hair some more and then let his hand caress my neck.

"You have a stupid neck," Bounce blurted out suddenly, making me wonder about his sanity.

"So do you!" I shot back, pushing his knees.

Calmly and slowly, in a low tone, he responded, "Did I push you?" Then he pushed me back.

I retaliated, pushing him so hard that he fell off balance.

He recovered and pushed me back using more force.

The taller one continued in his dance ritual.

"I wanna __-u-c-k…I want some l-e-g," he chanted and then suddenly, without warning, hit me hard on my head, totally alarming me.

"Dawwg, Felicia, why you do me like that?" he growled.

The shorter guy was still cringing down in the corner where the taller one had kicked him.

"He is always picking on somebody," he wailed as he shielded his face.

"Yeah," I added, then I had to duck as the elder tousled my hair so badly that it looked much worse than when Bounce raked his hand through it.

Quickly, the shorter guy jumps up out of the corner and dares the taller.

"You hit me again and I'll…"

As he threatens, he grabs a rolled newspaper out of his back pocket and squarely faces his opponent.

By now it is about 9:30 p.m. and I am feeling like I have roused a wounded lion and am in danger of being torn apart. I had no intentions of leaving though. Bounce and I were here first. It's the intruders who should leave.

Suddenly my father came through the double building doors and quickly assessed my predicament. His naïve and silly daughter was alone in a building foyer at night with three street-wise, teenage boys. Without much of a greeting, and glancing cautiously at the boys he spoke into the air in a dry, tense manner.

"Get upstairs, Fulisha."

I felt belittled. He hardly looked at me and never spends any time with me, now he thought nothing of bossing me around at will and depriving me of my need for social interaction!

I didn't move right away, but after Dad had ascended the first flight of steps, I obeyed and followed him. He said nothing more to me that evening, and I went straight to my room. Though I may not have appreciated it then, he acted like a father to me that night.

As the days grew darker, my blissful relationship with Bounce "just up and died" in the bitter January cold. Even though there was only one high school in Mount Vernon, I never saw him in any classroom, hallway, or cafeteria, or on any school bus. If I was supposed to be even *one* of his girlfriends, why didn't we ever date or spend time together in places other than the hallway? Why didn't he ask me out to a dance, or to the movies or to a restaurant? I had to face the fact that I really didn't mean much to him and that his declared "love" for me had turned into something else.

One day after school, he was unusually eager to talk to me for a few minutes out in the hallway. Since he told me that he had to ask a very important question, I was very interested and sat down beside him on the top step of the stairway. He fumbled about trying to find words and laughed at his own inability to say what was on his mind. It was so unlike him; he was always so confident and free in expressing himself.

He finally gave up, admitting, "I can't say it."

I knew then what he wanted and was disappointed and out the window went my hope for a meaningful conversation. What could a guy want from a girl that's too shameful to actually say to her face? I was insulted that he would even ask me. He had not spent any time with me in weeks, hardly ever communicated with me, spent no money on me, and now he was asking me for this? Nothing in my demeanor suggested to him that I was that kind of girl, except maybe he saw a weakness in me.

Since he could not be direct, and because I wanted to end the demeaning conversation, I made it easy for him. I asked him a series of yes/no questions that would point out the obvious.

"Is it something you want me to do with you?"

"Yes," he replied.

"Is it something we do alone?"

"Yes."

"Is it something we do in the dark?"

"Yes." He seemed relieved that I had figured it out. He was salivating over the idea that I'd give in to what he wanted, without even giving me the courtesy of direct eye contact, complimentary words, the promise of love, a cheap ring or even a hot dog and a soda. He didn't care about *me*.

He just wanted sex, which was totally out of the question. I knew from my Bible reading what Jesus had to say on the topic; and I could definitely trust *His Words*. I was determined to follow God's will and do what He said—to wait until I was married. Besides, my goal in life was to be loved. Allowing Bounce to use my body to satisfy his urges, without making any real commitment to me, would not make me feel loved and valued, but the very opposite.

I learned a bit about love from the Bible stories I read. I considered what happened with Tamar, David's daughter (2 Samuel 13). Her half-brother Amnon was so desperately in love with her that he forced her to "lay" with him. His love completely vanished the next morning, proving that it was just *lust* that he felt. I listened to songs like "Reasons" by Earth, Wind and Fire. I knew that for a guy, sex did not mean love, but waiting patiently for the marriage day did. I read enough about girls being used for sex and having their hearts broken. I remembered how God's strong Holy Spirit warned me about promiscuity years ago. But most of all, I knew that God's word simply said to wait until marriage before having sex. With strength and resoluteness I didn't know I possessed, I got up from the staircase to leave.

"No, I can't," I said as I walked away from him.

I let the door to our apartment close harder than normal. That was the last time for a long time that I was so sure of myself.

During our next encounter, he demanded an explanation for my refusal. I realized then that I didn't have the self-confidence to argue my point. I simply said "I can't" again. When he pressed for a reason, I went into the apartment to my bedroom and returned with a sticker I had received from an inspirational literature company. It was a little larger than a postage stamp and depicted a soft, beautiful, color portrait of Jesus. I held it out so Bounce could *see* my reason for resisting if he could not *hear* it.

It didn't convince him. He snatched the sticker from my hand, crumpled it and indignantly threw it down. Shocked that he could just throw God to the floor, I stood there for a moment. Then I bent down to pick up my stamp. I was no good at explaining my faith. In my heart, however, I was determined to not give in. Our relationship remained a series of loose, strained encounters that only lasted a few minutes or seconds as we crossed each other's paths in the building. He stopped pressing the issue.

I busied myself with school, church and track that year. I still had a weakness, however, for Bounce's charm. One Sunday in April, he and I were exchanging words in the hall. Mom needed me to make her bed, so she invited him into our apartment to sit in the living room while I worked. When I finished the bed, I joined him and put on some records such as Barry White's *Never Gonna Give You Up* and *Show and Tell*. After listening to records, we got out a photo album. I showed him a picture of himself shooting basketball. He took the album from me, but I hassled to get it back. I didn't want him to see all my "ugly" pictures. We finally settled down to look at the pictures together, but I kept telling him to turn the page to avoid seeing the pictures of me.

"Why don't you go over to the other couch?" he calmly suggested.

We laughed. Soon I had to walk Frisky, and Bounce went his way. I wished we had more simple times together like that.

My mom told me she didn't like him. She could sometimes hear him punch the wall outside our apartment when I spent time with him in the hallway. Sometimes he would threaten to hit me but he'd always hit the wall instead. I was hanging on to those words he first captured me with and I trusted that way down deep inside he still loved me.

Future meetings with him became more complicated. I was flattered sometime later when he asked again for a kiss and I relented. I missed his attention. When he kissed me, he burped and I could smell milk on his breath then he seductively moved his hips around until it was more than a simple kiss. It was subtle move and it had opened up a new pattern in our relationship.

Over the next two years, I would see him only occasionally. During those times, though I wanted to talk, he wanted only to kiss, and it got to the point where I gave in a lot more than I wanted to in hopes that he would spend time talking to me. It didn't work; after he was done kissing, he quickly left. In retrospect, I am ashamed that I allowed him to treat me that way, but I justified my action thinking that one day we would be married. He respected my values because in the beginning he did not press to go all the way.

By the time we were close to sixteen, Bounce had become more tense and withdrawn. When we kissed he became more aggressive, trying to take what I didn't want to give. I was getting sick of his forcefulness and started to resist him. I put up one last struggle against him that ended his efforts. I got a call from him the next day.

"I got scratched yesterday and it's all your fault!" he said. "But I'm gonna let you off the hook."

"Really, you got scratched?" I asked, wondering how that happened but pleased that he actually took time to call me.

"Yeah, and I was thinking about coming over there and making you pay. You made me scratch myself on my zipper. I was planning on giving you a taste of your own medicine, but decided not to. You're lucky I'm letting you off the hook."

"What? I didn't do anything," I said, feeling horrible that I meant so little to him that he was thinking of hurting me…for something that was his own fault.

"Yeah, I know you didn't do it on purpose, so that's why I'm letting you off the hook."

I didn't put him straight, I didn't tell him a thing or two. I just felt dejected. He said a few more words and then hung up the phone

Soon afterwards he and his family moved away; he left without saying good-bye. At first I was relieved that I would not have to confront his arrogance and forcefulness again. But as the months went by and my loneliness increased, I began to miss him. My longing to see him grew until it clouded my memory and I all I could remember were the good times, the early times, the laughs, the loving words. I felt I had lost the only man in the world who paid any attention to me on a regular basis.

I turned to the only source of help I knew. I began to pray to the Lord, begging Jesus to bring back to me the man I loved and lost. As the years passed and the memories grew fainter, I continually pleaded with the Lord Jesus to give me a sign that Bounce would come back and marry me.

The Lord always answers His children's cries. In fact, He answered me three times, each response in the form of a dream. The three dreams said very clearly, "No way," "Absolutely not," and "Get over it." They were very consistent and simple in their message and I could not forget them.

The first was a clear view of Bounce's handsome, boyish, round face hanging midair before me. He was looking directly at me with bright sparkling eyes but he did not act as I hoped. Instead of smiling lovingly at me, he laughed mockingly. Then his image quickly faded away as I cringed in hurt.

The second dream portrayed him galloping on a beautiful white horse towards me. When he was within my reach, I was prepared for him to lean over to gather me up into his arms. He looked down at me with a mischievous smirk on his face. I was so elated to see him, thinking of myself as his future bride, that I stretched out my arms to be lifted up. In response, he let out a hideous, cold-hearted laugh, and then galloped speedily away, almost trampling me in the process.

A third dream echoed the same answer as the first two. Mom told me that I had a phone call from Bounce. I excitedly reached for the phone to speak to him, but when I put the receiver to my ear, all I heard were revolting, evil voices that gave me chills. I slammed the phone down and stared at the receiver in a state of shock.

These three dreams were spread out over a period of about a year, occurring at different times as I continued praying. The Lord was clearly saying "no," but I wasn't listening. It was not the answer I wanted so I decided that the dreams were not from God. They were simply fragments of my own subconscious fears. I continued to beg the Lord to send Bounce back to me.

While I allowed myself to be fooled by an illusion, I missed out on some healthy dating experiences with respectable young men. I rejected two high school gentlemen who treated me like a lady. I was too busy clinging fast to a memory of a charming young boy with the bounce in his step who said he'd marry me. None of the others were like him. They were not exciting, independent, adventurous, cocky and elusive like the guy I was attracted to. The other prospects paled in comparison to Bounce even though they may have had so much more to offer. I suppose when one is not used to quality, even a showy clay pot can seem like a treasure. So in the next few years, while normal teenagers were out socializing and having fun, I spent hours in my room howling up to heaven.

Youthful convictions are hard to kill; but the Heavenly Father's love is even more stubborn.

Chapter 11

A House Falls

"And the rain descended, and the floods came, and the winds blew, and beat upon that house; and it fell; and great was the fall of it."
Matthew 7: 27 (King James Version)

Life is full of paradoxes. While I was grasping tightly to foggy memories, Dad was allowing something real to slip through his fingers. Apparently, neither Dad nor I knew who on earth to cling to. Dad was losing his wife, who was a good woman, and in retrospect, the best thing that ever happened to him, and I was desperately clinging to someone who was so wrong for me. I guess I was like my father in some ways.

My parents' verbal disagreements continued and the pattern was always the same. Mom demanded money for clothes, food and other needs. Dad refused to release it and Mom started nagging. Then Dad erupted in anger, threatened to hurt her physically and Mom quieted down…for the moment. Dad stormed out of the house and Mom held the household together until she was forced to ask for his help again.

What made matters worse was that Dad did not help with the children or the household chores. Exhausted from her job, the care of three children and housework, Mom had little sympathy for Dad. She argued that these were his children also and constantly reminded him of his responsibility to help care for them. Mom's quick tongue was never laced with expletives, but her continual words were enough to make his temper flare.

The verbal fights were carried on in front of us. Often, if she gave us instructions while he was present, he would belittle her in front of us, telling us, "You don't have to listen to that witch! She's nothing but a witch."

Mom was no "witch" and I knew Daddy was wrong to accuse her so. His calling her that did much harm because it provided an excuse to rebel against the one who was constantly looking after us. It was Mom who did everything for us, taking us to doctors, dentists, church functions, school functions, shopping, hairdressers and barbers. She was the one who kept the house clean and did our laundry. She was the one who put toys under the Christmas tree. She put together the fun birthday parties with delicious chicken salad sandwiches, cut up into fours, with the crust taken off. We had plenty of cookies, sugar cereals and Kool-Aid in the food closets due to her efforts. She was always there for us, loving, caring and sacrificing. Therefore, instead of having any power, his words just sounded mean to me. He was trying to hurt Mom. I knew that he had no intention of replacing the "mothering" he tried to snatch from us.

Mom told me years later that when she complained to someone about her predicament, she was advised to send us children down to live with her mother in Virginia. She was repulsed by the idea. She could never dump her children off on her mother. She found a way to manage and take care of her kids even if it meant working nights or two jobs, and that is what she did for a while.

Mom brought Valerie (age 9) and me (age 7) pretty summers dresses.

We always dressed up for Easter. Valerie is 10, Neil is 3 and I am 8

Valerie and me

Spending time in my Grandmother Field's yard (summer 1974)

Dad stayed with us until June of 1974. His company, Litton, moved from Long Island, New York, to Maryland, and Daddy followed his employer three hundred miles away. I figured they offered him a good deal because he left without taking us. He bought one end of a duplex townhouse in Riverdale with a veteran's loan for $27,000. It had an adequate half yard, carport and driveway, a bath and a half, a small eat-in kitchen, a dining room/living room combination and three small bedrooms. It was on a street with a cul-de-sac at the end. It would have been nice for a family of five.

He left thinking we would follow him. Mom had no intentions of relocating with him so she remained in the apartment. She felt that this was God's way of answering her prayers to take him away. Once Dad realized that Mom was not going to follow him, he took her to court, telling the judge that he had provided a home for his wife and kids, but she refused to relocate. The judge had no sympathy for a woman who rejected the efforts of a hard-working African-American father trying to provide for his family and warned her that if she and the children did not join her husband, she would get no child support or alimony. Mother was determined not to take the risk of losing everything she had acquired since leaving Blackstone (her job, her church, her proximity to relatives and her apartment) by depending on Dad. She promptly went out and opened up a checking account to pay the bills out of her own earnings and never looked for any support from Dad.

I was relieved when Daddy left. Now the tension, conflict and arguments would leave with him and there would be peace in our home. Mom's authority would reign unchallenged and there would be serenity. I was wrong. Dad's absence left a huge void, and achieving peace and order in the home was more difficult than I imagined. Mom, left alone with three children, tried hard to make our broken family work. Neil was ten years old when Dad left us. I was fifteen and Valerie was seventeen. Valerie and Neil took Dad's leaving very hard. They missed him and were angry with Mom. They lost their tempers, disobeyed her and talked back. I was reclusive, depressed and oddly enough, a "miss-know-it-all." Rebellion and hormones were in full swing and Mom was the lone adult against three moody and emotionally wounded adolescents. Mom did the best she could to provide for us in spite of the emotional turmoil.

Because I loved Dad, I was happy for him; in fact we all were. Even Mom wished him no harm. I was proud that he purchased a home. That was my dad—always strong, independent and capable. I wished him well and really wanted him to succeed. At the same time, I sighed with relief that he was out of my life. Never again would he hurt me. I felt that now I had a chance to feel better about myself. I knew he would not seek after me, which was a good thing because his careless words and actions only made me feel worthless.

While I was enjoying the peace afforded by Dad's absence, Mom struggled to keep Valerie and Neil on course. Eventually, Valerie moved down to Maryland to live with Daddy for a few years. Years later, I learned from her that she had a taste of what I suspected would happen if you put yourself in Dad's care. She was neglected. He locked her out several times when she came home too late at night. She had no choice but to go home with the taxi driver or sleep out in some vacant lot. She doesn't talk much about her experiences down there except to admit that they were not good. Valerie and Mom are closer today than ever.

Neil spent some summers with Dad. Since he was five years my junior, I lost contact with him and he did not talk of his time with Dad. I doubt if they were the positive ones that a young man needed from his father. Valerie and Neil eventually came back to live with Mom. Neil has since found an apartment of his own, turned to the Lord and is an active member of a vibrant church.

I spent a guarded week or two with Dad during the summer when I was sixteen years old. While I was there, I knew that I had to fend for myself, but at least I was of age and prepared for the loneliness. I did a lot of cooking, cleaning and walking to the nearby shopping center on my own. I was alone so often I couldn't imagine living an extended amount of time with him.

After my parents separated, Dad always visited us during the holidays. He stayed with one of his relatives, often popping in unexpectedly. Mom let him come by the apartment to see us. I had prepared for one of his visits. I was going to show him God's Word and help him to see the error of his ways. I had recently discovered a Bible verse that says, *"But if any provide not for his own, and specially for those of his own house, he hath denied the faith, and is worse than an infidel" (1 Timothy 5:8)*. I thought that if I showed this scripture to Dad, he would receive God's words with humility and repent. I was not prepared for his reaction.

When I read him the text, he was very defensive and declared, "What are you talking about?!! I provide for my family!"

"But, Dad, you don't give us much money…you don't buy us clothes…"

"I provide for my family! I brought you all a house in Maryland! Ya'll wouldn't come!"

I was shocked that he thought he was a good provider. I was shocked that he thought he bought *us* a house. I was shocked that he expected us to come. I don't remember him asking me to go. I was confused and tried to figure out what to say next. Did he think that we had abandoned *him* by not following? Would you not treat someone better if you wanted them to follow you? I couldn't think of anything else to say. Dad did not see my point at all so the discussion ended there. I concluded that I just could not understand his way of thinking. It seemed like years passed before I saw him again.

I graduated from high school in 1977. Mom was there. Dad was not. I looked like a little old woman in one of the photographs with an unflattering dress, skinny legs, awkward glasses and flat hairdo. Well, at least I didn't have to look at myself. I was ready to find employment and to start helping Mom with the finances.

Mom would not hear of it and insisted that I attend college.

I didn't want to go to college, burdening Mom with that huge financial load. Besides, I had no idea of what I wanted to study and could not make up my mind on a career. I was interested in teaching, but simply did not have the confidence to face a classroom full of children. I was interested in nursing, but Mom was against it. Having been a nurse's aid she felt it would be too laborious.

However, my mom had a stronger will than I and a quicker tongue. She won that battle easily. Upon her word and the advice of my high school counselor, I applied to Colgate University and was accepted as a University Scholar.

The University Scholars Program at Colgate was designed to help qualified minority students compete on the college level. It required attendance in the summer before the freshman year, during which we earned credits for two core courses, math and English, and adjusted to campus life.

Along with the other University Scholars gathered at the Port Authority bus station, I boarded the chartered bus to Hamilton, New York, in June of 1977, to report to Colgate as directed.

Chapter 12

A Beautiful Place

"He that loveth his life shall lose it; and he that hateth his life in this world shall keep it unto life eternal."
John 12:25 (King James Version)

I was glad to have the opportunity to escape to a different world. I still longed for the young man who said he'd marry me, but he was somewhere in the world not even thinking of me. It was good to be in a place where I could begin to forget, for here there was little to remind me of him. I was now surrounded by beauty I rarely saw—rolling, green hills, cows grazing in pastures, endless sky and most excitingly a whole new pool of educated and handsome African-American men.

Romance was everywhere among the small group of minorities who had a light academic load in a resort-like place during the balmy days of summer. Lakes, ponds and hiking trails were within walking distance, so we students enjoyed idyllic conditions perfect for falling in love. The town, about a mile away, was quaint and quiet. Beyond the campus and town were acres of dairy farms, so if you were a student without a car like the majority of the minorities, you stayed on campus and found diversions there.

Of course, there was little domestic work to do, only an occasional load of laundry. Hot meals were served three times a day. The only catch was that you had to walk down a steep hill, which was more like an advanced ski slope, nicknamed "Killer Hill." You could not get to the dining hall from the freshman dorms without dealing with that hill. But we were young and quite capable of the challenge and we enjoyed the view from the top. I don't recall seeing many professors walk that hill.

I was captivated by the self-assured, debonair manners of a brown-skinned guy. He was of average height, had a muscular body and a handsome face. His skin was flawless and the color of dark cocoa. He, a sharp dresser, walked with rhythm and confidence and when he smiled, clean neat teeth broadcasted impeccable hygiene.

As our paths crossed, he showed approval, winking and smiling. The high point of our encounters occurred at a party in the dorm lounge. As I sat against the wall, which I usually did at these parties, he walked over to me and held out his hand, offering me a dance—during a slow song! I think it was Earth, Wind and Fire's "Reasons." I could hardly believe it—that he had chosen me. I sighed in his arms, thoroughly enjoying being in the embrace of this very fine man. I rested my head on his shoulder and inhaled the sweet aroma of his cologne. With him, I could forget about Bounce. As it turned out, I didn't get a chance. After the dance, he resumed his usual distance. I was not in the habit of chasing a man so he remained a familiar stranger to me. I completed the summer requirement and went home to prepare to return for the fall semester.

When I returned in September, I found myself in a dormitory full of white strangers. My room was not near any of the students I had met over the summer. The administration had scattered us African Americans all over campus in different buildings. Now I learned what it meant to feel out of place.

My roommate was a friendly, cheerful young woman who called her boyfriend frequently throughout the week, and every weekend or so he visited her. They seemed happy, carefree and in love, just like in the movies. She was very nice to me and I liked her, but we drifted apart after that first semester. Though she and some of the other girls in my dorm were very friendly, I didn't really fit in. Many of them seemed to have doting parents, tons of comfort items for their rooms, boyfriends, confidence, and a daredevil approach to life. There were beer parties going on all around me, and one of the hottest songs played in the dorms was by the Bee Gees—"Staying Alive!"

I found camaraderie at mealtimes, when I had the opportunity to reunite with my summertime friends. At one meal before the Christmas break, the fine young man I danced with gave his final assessment of me. He was sitting across from me in the cafeteria at dinnertime and blurted out that I was ugly in front of everyone. At that time, I guess I deserved it. I didn't wear make-up and I had given up on my hair which hadn't been touched by a beautician in several months.

I slipped out of the cafeteria crushed, feeling totally discouraged. Rejection still followed me, all the way up to Colgate. I couldn't seem to avoid it. I seemed doomed as a woman who would never find love. I walked back to my dorm room, eyes welling up with tears. I avoided as many people as I could over the next few weeks, tending only to my classes and course work.

Being alone in a cold, heartless world can work wonders if it pushes you in the right direction. One night, despair overwhelmed me. I felt such depression and discouragement coming upon me that if I didn't leave the room, my roommate would have to witness my uncontrollable, unexplainable sobbing. I could not burden her with my depression. She was on her bed, lying peaceably on her belly, as she curled up her legs and read a book, totally unaware of the torment building inside of me.

I hurried out into the night and walked up the parking lot towards the top of a small hill. It was a beautiful night, with mild temperatures and a clear sky full of stars. I stood still looking up. My heart was filled with despondency. I was at the end of myself, full of hopelessness and despair. I wanted to give up and go on to heaven. Life on this earth without love was too much for me to bear and I was helpless to change my situation.

Heaven is not like this, I thought. It's a beautiful place full of God's love, goodness and happiness. I wanted to be there. Since I was nowhere near death, I could only stand in the presence of my God with a broken heart, knowing that He was there and that He cared. How I wished I could be with Him. In my heart, I talked to the Lord, thinking, "Lord, I wish I could just be with you." Self-pity had me completely cast down.

As the tears began to fall, the Lord suddenly spoke. His words were not audible by the ear, but they were stronger and clearer than anything I ever heard. They came from a place I never paid attention to before, a place not in my head, where my thoughts come from, but from a place deep within my upper body, somewhere beyond the heart, between the ribs, deep inside. It was the place of the human spirit where God's Spirit dwells.

The voice was masculine, deep and very firm:

"Felicia, if you love me, you must take up your cross daily and follow me."

I knew instantly who it was who spoke to me. Jesus spoke the very same words in the book of Matthew: *"Then said Jesus unto his disciples, If any man will come after me, let him deny himself, and take up his cross, and follow me" (Matthew 16:24).* And in the book of Luke: *"And he said to them all, If any man will come after me, let him deny himself; and take up his cross daily and follow me" (Luke 9:23).* My spirit revived and my heart jumped for joy that the Lord was there to comfort me.

Afterwards my mind was filled with questions. I was a little offended by the "if." I thought, Lord, you know I love you, and just to prove it, I am going to do as you say, take up my cross and follow you. But what exactly does that mean?

Just as quickly as He dropped those words into my spirit, the silence of the night returned. But my heart was no longer heavy. Jesus knew that I lacked the conviction that my life on this earth was worthwhile, so that night He gave me the boost I needed.

Since He answered me no more, I had to decide what his words really meant. I figured the Lord wanted me to change churches, to leave the Baptist one in which I grew up and join a Pentecostal church that my new "saved" hairdresser had been telling me about. That was the only decision that was pending in my life at that time. Okay, I could do that, although I would have to endure Mom's objections. She said that she "was born a Baptist and would die a Baptist" and she expected me to do the same.

From a perspective of thirty years later, I have a better understanding of what the Lord was telling me. Joining the Pentecostal church was the short-term goal, but the Lord also was giving me something to work on for the long term. Translated into my own words, the Lord's long-term goal for me was, "Enough with the pity parties, already! Just trust in *Me*!" Rather than focusing on me—how I was so rejected, ignored, insulted, lonely and unpopular—I needed to forget about myself and concentrate on Him! He was letting me know that rejection was part of the cross I had to bear and that good would come out of it. He, as my example, suffered infinitely worse, being rejected, scorned, despised, ridiculed and finally unjustly condemned to carry a literal cross to a torturous death, and it is a gross understatement to say that good came out His submission to the purposes of God! I just needed to follow in His footsteps and carry my cross without the whining and self-pity, knowing that God is faithful to work everything for our good. It would be a few more months before I got that message.

Though I didn't understand all of the implications of His words right away, I returned to my dorm room elated by a another revelation. I didn't have to look up to the sky anymore to talk to God. He wasn't up there. He had been living on the inside of me all along ever since I had asked Him into my heart, as repulsive as I thought I was. I figured that I could not have been that horrid if God Himself moved in. I was uplifted for it was impossible to think poorly of myself once I understood that I was a temple of the Living God!

I slept very peacefully that night.

* * *

During college break, back in Mount Vernon, I joined a Pentecostal church and became very active. It was a good church for me at that time. Like the Baptist church it was within walking distance, yet it offered practical teaching on how to live as a Christian. The pastor preached about real issues of temptation facing young people.

I was a young and single woman facing many opportunities to indulge in the sensual life. I needed the humorous, lively and relevant preaching the pastor and his wife specialized in. Pastor openly rebuked fornication, adultery, alcohol consumption, drug abuse, smoking, swearing, cursing, and promiscuity as he strutted animatedly from one side of the pulpit to the other and then up and down the aisle. I agreed with his warnings to abstain from activities on this list. It was good to finally hear what I had read in the Bible preached from the pulpit. I was finally in a church that preached what made sense to me—abstinence!

For a while I loved it there. The pastor was dynamic and funny, and participating in the choir was an awesome experience. I was a second soprano and enjoyed the jubilant, heartfelt songs of praise. We didn't have many men in the choir, or in the church for that matter, but two or three guys could make their bass or baritone voices heard over thirty sopranos and altos. I was very busy as a church member, serving as a Sunday school teacher, Bible school teacher, fund raiser, and as a guest soloist or speaker during the Friday night evangelistic services. Though I did not agree with all of the denomination's doctrines, it was a good place for me to be at the time. My godly beautician, and the woman who led me to the church, wisely introduced me to a female member who was my age. I enjoyed a rich friendship with her because she was kind, sincere and very funny.

I also spent time with the hairdresser. After I had been a member for about a year, she and I ran off to various "Holy Ghost" camp meetings looking for a "fresh anointing" from God. Once we traveled to Brooklyn to a summertime tent meeting of a very popular evangelist who had a special gift for performing miracles. The evangelist started ministering, it seemed as though everyone except me was being blessed as he or she fell out into the sawdust under the power of God when the evangelist pointed in their direction and pronounced words of prophecy. I stood there watching with envy. When I got home, I closed my bedroom door, got down on the floor with my Bible and cried and prayed and sulked. Then I dared to accuse God. I thought, *See, God, even You don't love me.*

That ended the current and all future pity parties! I didn't have to read Psalm 145:9, because it leaped right off the page. God's Spirit quickened His word with so much power and authority that it felt like a slap on my face. *"GOD IS GOOD TO ALL!"* The emphasis was on the word "all," which included me. I got the message that time.

As time went by, the list of do's and don'ts in the Pentecostal church I attended got a bit too burdensome for me. In addition to the reasonable warnings against pre-marital sex, alcohol or smoking, it dragged on to forbid dancing, swimming in public, excessive jewelry, make-up, movies, pants on females, shorts or anything worn too short, sleeveless tops, spaghetti straps, open-toe shoes, nappy hair (I was doomed), and even a little wine for the stomach's sake. Now, I had already been saved or born again, had followed Jesus for some time now and read His Word. He accepted me as I was, wearing shorts and pants, and never convicted me about wearing them. He certainly convicted me about things—such as my thoughts and actions—the twisted stuff inside my heart. Just cleaning up my wretched insides and molding my pattern of thinking into His was a colossal job in itself. If you add my focusing on my bodily exterior to the list, the job of being a "saint" became too impossible for me. My salvation was a free gift of God and I wanted to keep it that way.

I submitted to the church's teachings as a member and to avoid offending my fellow believers, but I began to get into arguments with the leadership and members about grape juice, wine, sin and forgiveness. I started living a double life. When I rode my bike in the summer, I would sneak outside wearing shorts and hurry through Mount Vernon at top speed to avoid being seen by any of the other "saints." When I went off to college, I wore pants (it was much too cold in the hills of upstate New York during the winter to flirt with skirts). If anyone from the church saw me, I might be labeled as a "backslider"—even if I loved the Lord with all my heart.

As time went on, I became more and more uncomfortable in my church home. I didn't know the Lord was preparing me to leave just as He had prompted me to join.

Chapter 13

Grandma Fields

"But the godly will flourish like a palm tree and grow strong like the cedars of Lebanon. For they are transplanted into the Lord's own house. They flourish in the courts of our God. Even in old age they will still produce fruit; they will remain vital and green. They will declare, 'The LORD is just! He is my rock! There is nothing but goodness in him!'"
Psalm 92:12-15 (NLT)

The Christmas/winter break at Colgate was called the January Project. Three of the four Januaries during my years at Colgate had to be spent studying, but you could choose any topic that caught your interest. In January 1978, I chose gerontology.

I checked out a few library books on old age, packed my bags and hopped on a bus to Blackstone. My plan had a twofold purpose. I would satisfy the school requirement for the January Project and provide my grandmother, who was eighty-two at the time, with some much-needed company during the coldest and loneliest time of the year. Her faith in the Lord, her godly demeanor and the beautiful way in which she aged was such an inspiration to me that I always wanted to spend more time with her. I was thrilled to have the opportunity to do just that.

As Grandmother grew older, her hair turned a beautiful blend of peppered silver. Her skin remained smooth and her eyes never lost their twinkle. Her speech was filled with praise and thanksgiving. "I thank the Good Lord for all of my blessings." She didn't fear death but looked forward to "going home." She was so positive that I wanted to hang around her and learn more of her secrets of being happy and content. Even as a widow in her seventies she was still very attractive. I watched her enjoy a little romance as she "kept company" with an elderly gentleman by the name of Mr. Stokes. He died shortly after their relationship developed.

Her greatest testimony was that "God had brought her from a mighty long way." I waited for the right time to ask her about her journey. As we lay in the pitch darkness one night, she on the twin bed and I on the full-size bed, she satisfied my curiosity by telling me about a dream she had of her second husband. In this dream God showed her a picture of the man she would marry. She saw a brown, round-faced man with kind eyes. That man was John Fields, who was tall and brown with a round face, broad nose and full lips. I was amazed and encouraged by that dream and wanted God to do the same thing for me. After hearing my grandmother's account I decided that I too would look for my brown, round-faced man.

As part of the study, I was required to keep a journal of notes on the books I read. To make the journal more interesting and meaningful to me, I added my observations of that time I spent with Grandmother.

* * *

It is January 6, 1978, and finally I am about to leave for Virginia. My study should continue with increased diligence and enthusiasm, for I will be in such a quiet surrounding that if no genuine initiative is there to push me to study, boredom will.

Blackstone, Virginia, is very rural; no city is around for at least thirty miles, and that is Petersburg. The nearest hospital is Richmond, sixty miles away. Grandma's little five-room; cinder-block home is seven miles along a narrow twisting road from the small commercial area of Blackstone. Several banks, grocery stores and drug stores line the two-block-long downtown area. A few churches are scattered here and there; there are no movie theatres or big shopping centers. From where we were, on Route 2, no car meant not being able to get about, to anywhere. We had no car; I should study well.

It's only recently that Grandma has had any significant signs of aging. Her hair is a mixture of black and gray, her eyes a bit weak, but not needing glasses, her hearing bad at times, but these small ailments hardly stopped her from attending church services weekly in a clean, crisp, white usher dress.

She would always be the first one ready, sitting vigilantly at the window patiently watching us: my mom scrambling through the suitcase for a pair of pantyhose, my aunt combing my little cousin's hair telling her to stop screaming so; and my older cousins and I trying out difference scents of powders and perfumes. "Ugh, that stinks! Mmm, can you smell this on me?"

Soon, a car would slowly drive up the road and stop in front of the house, right up near the mailbox, under the tall pines and oak tree. Grandma would exclaim, "You all come on, now, he's here!" Uncle would reinforce Grandma's statement with a polite blow of his horn, and we'd all scramble out of the house grabbing our pocketbooks and a last-minute handful of tissues.

Grandmother Fields, all dressed up and ready to go, poses for the camera in her front yard.

In church, the grown-ups would file in and take their respective pews. We girl cousins would crowd in the back rows near the windows and the boys. Grandma would sit up front. After a while, someone would begin to sing and soon the whole church would join in. Grandma would begin a song, too, to my surprise, and even stand up to testify! She thanked God for the many blessings He had given her. At the end of service, everyone would greet Grandma with smiles and kisses. Last year, her church gave her a wonderful testimonial service for all the years of dedicated service she gave.

Aging didn't stop Grandma from going into town with us. I loved those rides into town. We went before noon, bright and early. Uncle would drive relaxingly along the scenic country route, taking the well-known curves with precision and ease at forty miles per hour, while I sucked in the warm air pouring through the open window. In town, Grandma would go with us from one five and ten store to another, buying whatever we needed. She even helped with the cooking and wash, which was done by hand, at home. In the winter, when we were not with her, it was her habit to carry blocks of wood Uncle had chopped into the house to fuel the only source of heat, the wood-burning stove. Grandma seemed just as young as the rest of us.

When she was eighty-one, it seemed that time had to give her a stinging reminder of her mortality. One day in the winter of 1977, Grandma was carrying into the house some blocks of wood when suddenly a sharp pain struck her in the chest traveling down her left arm. She dropped the wood, unable to carry it due to the pain and discomfort. From that point on, it was low fat, no-salt foods, less work and lots of rest.

Grandma is fine now. She has spells of tiredness, especially during the winter. A cold, along with personal worries seem to make her tired, but she continues in faith and love, always willing to give a smile and to help as best she can. She is extremely wise, knowing her limitations and the ways of people. I love to listen to her when she feels like talking. I have never heard her denounce anyone, complain about her circumstances, gossip or curse. She uses her voice to praise her Lord and Savior and to exalt, admonish, lift up and encourage.

On the night of Sunday, January 9, 1978, Grandma was in a talking mood. We began talking about old times. I began to become very interested in knowing exactly who so and so was, and how he or she was related to me. Grandma would confuse me calling names of relatives I didn't know existed.

I thought that I knew or had heard of everyone in the family, but how wrong I was. I could never know all, much of it is lost and the rest is too huge and still growing.

She recalled everyone she could remember as vividly as if they were living now. It made me happy to witness her sharp mind. She had eleven children; two died about the age of twenty, the others are alive. Her first child was born in 1916, when she was twenty-one years old. She even remembered her grandparents, Robert and Anna Harper, saying, "he was a short man, shorter than Grandma, short and stout. Grandma was tall and stout."

As I was drawing the family tree and placing the birth year near the appropriate name, it filled me with wonder to realize that Grandma was born in 1895. I said that she have must have gone through some kind of history! I was delighted when she related to me how she felt about her first ride in a car.

"Your Aunt Margaret (her first child) was twelve months old. Mathis and I used to work for a white man, and he owned a T-Model Ford. We were at church, Mathis and I, on the church ground waiting for him to come and pick us up for work. He came to meet us in his T-Model Ford; folks were looking. It was the only car in the yard among horses and buggies. I was a big shot that day. I got in that car, sat back and thought I was something. Yes, I was a big shot that day. Shucks!"

"And what happened?" I asked, amused and tickled at the idea of Grandma showing off.

"I rode in it, but the road was so bumpy and hilly; that car bounced and shook me up so, I was just as sore the next day. I said that's the last time I'll ride in a car. You go down the gully, up the hill, over the bumps. That car really shook me up. I wasn't any more big shot."

"You weren't going to ride in any more cars?" I asked.

"That's what I said, but now the roads are smooth now. Yes, the road is good now."

"No more T-Model Ford's around here now!" I commented.

"No, they have gone out of style," Uncle James mused.

That year was 1921, and here it is 1978. How sound she still is at eighty-two. Her faith in God impressed me most. She told me that when she was alone and depressed, she would read "a little something about her Jesus" and that would keep her going.

"Thank you, Jesus," she said. "Thank the Lord, thank Him for my health, and this little food I have to eat. Some people have none. He has really done good things for me, and when I die it will be alright because I'm going home to Jesus my Lord!"

* * *

I was glad I spent time with Grandmother that January, for afterwards I did not have another chance. That summer, Grandma suffered a major stroke, lost her independence and had to move into a nursing home in town where she lived for another thirteen years.

Grandmother Fields (89 years old) sat in her yard one of the visits back to her house from the nursing home

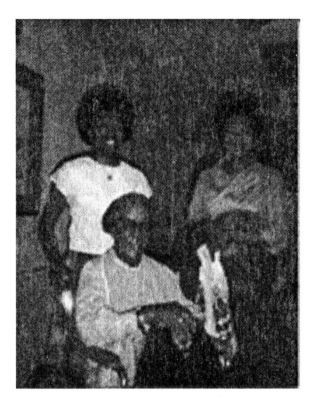

Mom, Grandmother Fields and I in the nursing home.

She was an exemplary resident at the nursing home. She continued to be positive and was often chosen to say a morning blessing over the intercom system. She even participated in and won a rocking chair marathon! The staff was graced by her cheery smiles and kind words. Aunt Mary explained to me years later that Grandmother suffered from a bladder infection while there at the nursing home and had so much faith that she refused an operation and trusted God to heal her. It eventually cleared up.

When she died in August of 1991 at the age of ninety-six, I had no doubt that she went home to paradise to be with her Lord. I now consider that time with her during a bitter January one of my warmest memories. I plant marigolds in my garden in memory of her.

Chapter 14

Eyes of Grace

"…Humans look at outward appearances, but the Lord looks into the heart."
1 Samuel 16:7 (GOD'S WORD)

My sophomore year at Colgate was more enjoyable than the first because I roomed with people with whom I had more in common. My roommates were all minority women, some of whom I had met during sub-frosh summer. There were four of us girls in a room called a quad. Beverly, born in Jamaica, and I were in one bedroom. A Chinese and a local African American from the town of Rome slept in the other.

Beverly and I became close friends. Our mutual commitment to Jesus gave us a deep respect for one another. She was in love with Eric, who would call every weekend. I remember her joy when she was called to the pay phone out in the hall. She would laugh and jump up and down like a toddler, clapping and exclaiming, "Oh, Felicia, it's Eric!" before rushing to the phone. I admired her because she had a good man who loved her, knew what she wanted and had the confidence to go after it. Later, she and Eric married and had two sons. She chose a career as a registered nurse and he became a pastor.

Beverly and I got involved with a group of Christians on campus called the Intra-Varsity Christian Fellowship. Hanging out with them encouraged me. It was predominantly a group of Caucasian believers, but they accepted me. The guys were enthusiastic about talking about the Lord, reading the Bible and saying short, simple prayers. The women were quiet and gentle. I went to the meetings frequently without Beverly, who seemed to prefer worshipping alone. I enjoyed many elements of the Intra-Varsity Christian Fellowship meetings, especially the cozy campfires on top of a hill and the soothing, live guitar music.

I had a short-lived crush on a junior during my sophomore year. I expressed interest in this guy because he reminded me of an uncle on my mother's side of the family whom I admired. He seemed gentle, kind and thoughtful. I wanted a man like Uncle Samuel, who was not only clearly handsome and intelligent, but more importantly totally devoted to his wife and four children.

I thought maybe this guy could be my "Uncle Samuel" He noticed me staring at him and his buddies urged him to talk to me. We met a few times and chatted about our former love lives, but most of the time, we had little to say and our moments together were filled with awkwardness. Our most interesting time together occurred when we were in a quad with another couple and someone brought up the subject of sex. I declared that I was waiting until I got married. That created all sorts of objections from the men and caused a lively and amusing debate.

After that, our meetings were pretty dull. I thought, well, since I really was not interested in this guy I could pretend he was someone I liked. My scheme did not go unnoticed. My thoughts were as clear as glass as we sat on the floor of my dorm room listening to Barry White's song "Ecstasy," a big hit at the time. As I looked into his eyes, I imagined that he was someone I loved. Reading me like a book, he smashed my fantasy by saying, "I'm not Bounce, Felicia." *Wow,* I thought; *this relationship is doomed.*

Later I found out that he complained to Walter Johnson that he "just couldn't get any." By that time, we had decided to go our separate ways, but the remark puzzled me. I never knew he was trying to "get" sex out of our relationship. Walter told me that he felt proud of me and said to himself, "Good for you, Felicia!" He didn't run back to tell me at the time suspecting that his comment would cause trouble. I was glad he eventually told me. You never know who is watching you.

I first took note of this tall, lanky guy named Walter on a sunny day in front of the college dining hall and I dismissed him at first sight. I observed his ill-fitting clothes, musty bicyclist's odor, untrimmed lopsided Afro, excessive cheerfulness and carefree stroll and instantly thought, *I could never marry that guy.* He was just too strange, inside and out. He walked about campus showing all of his front teeth. I couldn't understand how anyone could be so happy, so purely giddy. He acted as though this world was a wonderful place and he treated everyone in his path with ebullient greetings, including me. Now in my experience, either a guy was friendly because he was romantically interested or ignored me because he wasn't. Walter Johnson did not fit in either scenario. He was so far off my radar, I had no idea of how to read him.

I already had in mind what was best for me. I didn't know how to dress fashionably, but I wanted someone who did. Also, I was looking for a brown-skinned man. I was thinking of someone like a Kunte Kinte who was captured from his homeland, sold into bitter slavery and forced to begin his life alone in a cruel, hostile world simply because of his dark skin color. I read Alex Haley's book *Roots* with fascination and then watched Levar Burton in the movie version miniseries by the same name. Definitely someone of Mr. Burton's skin tone, or like the brown round-faced man in Grandmother's dream, would prove to be the best husband for me. In my mind, I was no match for a "pretty light-skinned black man" who was usually much higher up on the social ladder and who was the goal of countless aggressive women. Besides, light-skinned men like my dad did not take me seriously.

As I pointed to Walter's undesirable traits, four fingers pointed back at me. I had grown into a skinny nineteen-year-old, lacking curves, sporting a head full of damaged hair, wearing a size-10 shoe and oversized glasses with a prescription strong enough to distort my best facial feature. I was told by an ex-admirer that my skin was a beautiful brown, but I saw the blemishes. My ears were a little small and rounded like my dad's, and one stuck out a little. Out of respect for the church I attended, I wore no make-up. Out of ignorance, I used no healthy hair products and as a result of a poor self-image, my wardrobe was drab and dull. If my body was a size 8, I didn't even know it or try to show it. My clothes were a roomy size 10, and sometimes I wore even roomier size-11 and -12 hand-me-downs. It suited me just fine. I wanted to hide anyway. Mom told me I wore too many dark colors, but I did not want to attract any attention to myself, and was satisfied to wear clothes in the shades of brown and beige to best blend in with the furniture, the wall...a tree trunk. This was the "me" I presented to the world as my eyes scanned the horizon, searching intently for that immaculately groomed, confident, and handsome brown prince to come into my life and swoop me off to a world of happiness. Naturally, I kept praying. It would take a miracle.

Walter did not see a reject when he saw me. God gave him special eyes.

Our relationship began with teasing. Walter loved teasing the girls he befriended on campus. He would look at one and say, "I finally found you. Where have you been all my life?" She would tease him back replying, "I have been waiting for you, my love." They would both laugh. To another, he would ask, "Would you be one of my wives?" She would reply, "I need individualized attention." Some, playing along with his game, would say, "Okay!"

Then he tried to joke with me. We were walking in the same direction away from the dining hall. I had little to say to him since I did not strike up conversations with strange people I'd rather observe from a distance. He being friendly and playful, grabbed my hand, grinned and said, "Let's get married!" He picked the wrong person.

First of all, I was uncomfortable with physical contact. Secondly, I had a little pride and did not want to send the message to anyone watching that the only way I could possibly hold a guy's hand on campus was if it was some kind of a joke. Thirdly, upon hearing him mention marriage, I threw up defenses. I had been down that road before and was tired of men talking about marriage so flippantly. Marriage was a serious issue for me; it was my hope and one of my deepest desires, so don't play with me about marriage, because I am still waiting for that first guy to come back and fulfill his promise! Walter's little innocent game had turned disastrously sour and I communicated that fact to him with four words.

"Somebody might see us!" I warned as I yanked my hand away from his.

He was offended at the perceived insult, but politely replied, "I'm sure you could do worse!" He felt rejected; I was trying to protect myself. We went our separate ways not understanding each other's actions.

I bumped into Walter a few more times during that year at Colgate. Along with his book bag, he usually carried a camera ready to capture his darling peers on film, snapping album loads of posed and candid shots as he strolled merrily through the campus. To my suppressed horror, he took a few surprise shots of me and I worried that he would laugh and make fun of them with people who viewed his photo albums. Once I understood that he was genuinely sincere in collecting photos for his own memorabilia, I cooperated and even smiled for some of his pictures.

At another time, Beverly and I were walking towards the campus carrying cherished food supplies back from the store in town. We were taking turns holding the heaviest bag. After a good distance, we were approaching "Killer Hill" and felt exhausted just at the mere thought of climbing that hill with our load. Walter, gliding effortlessly toward us on his ten-speed bike, politely stopped to greet us, smiling from ear to ear. He seemed pleased at the opportunity before him. He offered us a deal—he would transport our package to our dorm room for a small fee—a kiss on the cheek from each one of us. To me, his request seemed very annoying and silly, but it was a small price to pay his assistance. Beverly and I agreed and gave him our bags.

When we met up with him in front of our dormitory, Beverly had no problem delivering her payment. I had issues with it and I tried to avoid paying, but Walter insisted that I keep my end of the bargain also and even bent down to offer me his cheek. Not wanting to waste time debating over something so petty, I reasoned it would be simpler just to comply. My lips touched his cheek so lightly and quickly that I could not see how he received any joy out of it, but he straightened up, flashed a wide grin, gave us a hearty "Thank you!" and rode contentedly off on his bike. Even after his kind gesture, I felt he was a strange, shallow and silly man.

During that year, I had many meaningful conversations with my peers, and one of those happened to involve Walter. On this occasion, a female peer and I sat in a dorm room and engaged in a discussion about marriage. Walter came in and joined us. My peer shared her willingness to live together like her parents. I admitted that I planned to marry a boyfriend I had long ago and hoped to see him again one day. Without telling them the details, I tried to explain why the man I expected to marry and I were not in touch with one another. I said that he had gone away suddenly and I did not know where, but one day we would meet again. My devotion to Bounce made no sense to Walter at all. He did not understand, knowing my standards, why I was even thinking about him, but discerned that this guy and I were not compatible. For the first time, I saw Walter look pensive and serious. He made no comment. It was such a remarkable scene that I sketched a picture of him sitting deep in thought. I thought it was really refreshing that he listened to and cared about what I said.

I did not see Walter often, but we sometimes were in the same place on Sunday mornings. He served as an usher at the University Church. I thought that was decent of him to volunteer his time for God, but for my taste, he still was not vocal enough about his faith in God.

My last memory of Walter at Colgate was towards the end of the year. I was walking from my dormitory toward "Killer Hill." As I approached the University Church near the top of the hill, I spotted Walter walking ahead. I decided to give him a taste of his own medicine of teasing people. Hiding behind a pillar on the church porch, I called out, "Walta!" He turned around to see who had called out his name and saw no one. He turned back and resumed walking. Again I called out his name, "Walta!" This time when he turned, he laughed, thoroughly enjoying this game by the invisible greeter. After another call he still could not locate me, so when he turned his back in my direction, I stepped out from behind the pillar and called his name again. He turned around, saw me and we both had a good laugh. That was my way of saying thanks and good-bye to a very good-natured acquaintance. We were both leaving Colgate; he was graduating and I was transferring out.

* * *

Academically, I did well at Colgate, but I could not decide on a major. I liked so many subjects and often desired to teach, but I did not have the guts to pursue anything. I had no career plan, no counseling and didn't seek out help. I tried to figure a career choice out on my own. I finally decided to do what I thought would be gentle on my fragile ego. Being as naïve as I was, I thought I might be able to serve the Lord on some foreign mission field and decided to transfer to a Christian college near my home. I completed the paperwork to transfer to the King's College in Briarcliff Manor. I picked this college after growing fond of listening to a devotional program aired on Christian radio by the college's president, Dr. Robert A. Cook.

I was running low on spending change and needed money for bus transportation home that spring. Mom encouraged me to write to Dad. I was reluctant to ask at first, but thought maybe Mom was right. There was a chance that Dad wouldn't mind helping out a bit since I hadn't asked him for anything in a long time and my current need for money as a full-time student was reasonable. I wrote him a letter. He wrote back:

> *2-22-79*
> *Dearest Daughter,*
> *I was delighted to hear from you. I am fine so far and in good health. Right now I am in the middle of a financial problem, but it should ease up soon. My money management has been bad lately. With your prayers and*

mine we cannot lose. I have a four-member family living with me now. The couple has two kids—boy and girl. They seem to be nice people. At least they are friendly. I'll send you more money soon, but keep in touch with me and remind me. Tell all of student friends hello for me. Take care of yourself. I will be in NY for Easter; hope to see you then. So long for now.

    With Love,
    Dad

It was a nice letter and the words were those of a loving dad, but I put it away discouraged. I was expecting more than the ten-dollar check he enclosed and wondered how I would get my things home.

The man who I misjudged as strange, shallow and silly proved to be the very opposite: grounded, thoughtful and wise. When it was time to leave in May, like many of my Colgate friends, I had to take a bus to New York City to get home. Without a car, I had no way of bringing my box of books, trunk, chair and lamp home. Walter decided that since he had use of his father's car, he would find a way to help his fellow peers. He rented a U-Haul trailer and charged ten dollars to transport people's things to their front door. He only asked that the person be at home on the date he planned to deliver his or her things. Some people didn't keep their side of the bargain and therefore Walter had to make multiple attempts to deliver the items, paying more for tolls and gas than he anticipated. Though he hoped the ten dollars would cover the cost of the service, he actually lost money in the deal. His service was a huge blessing to many of us students.

A few days after I arrived home in Mount Vernon, Walter called to say he was ready to deliver my trunk. He arrived on schedule. Upon meeting Walter, Mom was so overly impressed with the young man standing before her that I had to take note. She didn't treat any of the men I brought home so cordially. She enthusiastically chatted with Walter, grinning and laughing, and offered him a snack in her kitchen, use of her phone and more money to cover any extra expenses. He politely declined all except her offer to call his mother to let her know that he was on his way home. She thanked him profusely, grinning from ear to ear, until he got into the car. Then she joyously took time to lead him back to the highway in her car. I was intrigued by my mother's extreme hospitality.

I didn't know she could be so charming.

By the time Walter dropped off my things and left, my opinion of him had progressed from shallow guy to classy gentleman. Whoever won his heart would get a jewel. I didn't have a chance, so as he drove away he was dismissed from my mind. At least after years of silly infatuations, I was beginning to recognize gold.

Chapter 15

King's

"For I know the plans I have for you," says the Lord. "They are plans for good and not for disaster, to give you a future and a hope."
Jeremiah 29:11 (NLT)

My hope was rekindled. In the summer of 1979, before my junior year at the King's College, as I was walking down the street in Mount Vernon, a familiar figure was approaching me. It was someone who knew Bounce very well—his mother. I was so excited to see her! I detained her for a while in conversation with one goal—to milk her for information of his whereabouts. After a brief conversation, I walked away ecstatically carrying something very precious in my hands: Bounce's military address. He was stationed somewhere overseas. God had answered my prayers!

As soon as I had a chance, I wrote him a sheepish letter. I concealed my true intentions and simply let him know that I was thinking and praying for him. He wrote back. I was so relieved because he said he had become a Christian, wanted to see me again and asked for me to mail him a picture. I sent him the best one I could find, one in which I was not wearing glasses and had a decent hairstyle. I waited for his reply and for the day I would see him again.

In the meantime I was learning and growing at Kings. I enjoyed the chapel services, the guest speakers, songs and musicians. I took courses that fed my interest in the Bible such as Church History, Doctrines of the Christian Faith, the Writings of Saint Paul and a class about cults.

We had some dynamic motivational speakers. I still remember one visitor who addressed an informal gathering of students in the lounge of the main building. His words were alive, powerful and warm, like the crackling fire in the massive stone fireplace. He elegantly expounded on the principles of God's kingdom, in a clever, personal manner. His basic message was that the principles in God's Kingdom were opposite those of the world. If you want to be great, you have to willing to be the least. If you want to be first, you must be willing to be the last. If you want to live, you have to first die. If you want to be rich, you have to be willing to become poor. If you want to be happy, you must put God's desires before your own. He made it very obvious that God's ways are contrary to worldly wisdom. His words burned within my heart for I have seen these truths depicted out over and over again in life.

I also heard beautiful songs of praise and worship in the daily chapel service and at concerts presented by top Christian groups. One popular Christian music group of the 1980s was The Imperials, and they performed right there in the gymnasium.

I was also enjoying a brand-new group of friends at Kings. I was part of a group of Pentecostal students, mainly minorities, who met to pray and worship together. We sought after the indwelling of the Holy Spirit, heard prophecies from some of the members and prayed for each other. In our group was a Caucasian woman, from Westchester, NY, who was very bright. She went on to become an accountant. She was praying for a husband. There was an African American woman, with long relaxed hair, a beautiful square face, and gorgeous eyes. She was also praying for a husband and was studying to become a music teacher. Debbie was strong in the Lord and from Jamaica. She had a slender body frame, light skinned, with deep-set eyes, an oval face, high cheekbones and long thick curly hair, which she wore in a long ponytail. I'll always remember how she let the Lord use her during one of our prayer circles. One day, when about eight or nine of us women joined hands in a prayer, Debbie, in a calm and gentle voice, prophesized such loving and encouraging words that we spontaneously dropped hands and ran to our private corners to cry out to God. Gaye and another friend were also from Jamaica. Gaye was slender, brown skinned and round faced with beautiful doe-like eyes. She could make us laugh with her stories and animated manner. She was a very kind, generous and honest person and totally committed to the Lord. I marveled at her ability to share her struggles and feelings honestly with us. She became like a sister to me. Another peer was petite with a beautiful face. She was strong in her faith, and had definite career goals. She later became a very successful physical therapist. Tina, of Chinese descent, was bubbly, outgoing and bold. She enjoyed life with vigor. Together we all supported and prayed for each other.

The faith-building courses, uplifting speakers, musicians and God-fearing friends made my experience at King's a time of spiritual growth.

The downside of my time at King's was in seeing so many students who had no regard for the Lord and in being disappointed that I could not find a husband-to-be. But my faith grew at King's as I learned to wait through this period of silence and uncertainty. I strengthened my resolve to make Jesus the cornerstone of my life. I knew that somehow He would give me a bright future.

I pictured a brighter future with Daddy. When I arrive in that hospital room, Dad is going to weep. He'll apologize for all the things he didn't do, but should have. Then, it will be my turn to weep. I will tell him that I forgive him and we will embrace. His eyes will be filled with peace and joy. He will then give me wise direction on what to do next and be the father I always needed.

Chapter 16

A Summer Job

"The Lord protects the simple-hearted."
(Psalms 116:6, New International Version)

One day, at the end of my junior year at King's, a persuasive, short salesman, I'll call Mr. M, came to the college to offer an exciting opportunity to the mission-oriented students. He made the job as a door-to-door book salesperson sound as though it would meet every single one of our summer goals. We could avoid being lazy and idle, travel to distant places, meet new and wonderful people, experience faith-building challenges, witness to lost souls, build our self-esteem, exercise every day, run our very own business and make lots of money during one three-month summer break! I was not the only one convinced! Tina and I excitedly accepted the job along with another student I didn't know well who I'll call Jenny.

After the school year ended in May we loaded up the Volkswagen Rabbit Tina borrowed from her family and headed out to Nashville, Tennessee. There, we stayed at a hotel for a week, completing a company-paid training session. After learning sales tactics and memorizing the scripts for the three products we were to sell (a Bible study set, a medical encyclopedia and a cookbook) we were off to our designated sales area: Houston, Texas.

We were advised to first find a place to live by searching churches for people willing to host student book salespeople. Tina was the first to find accommodations. She had relatives living in an upscale residential area of Houston. Jenny and I were allowed to stay there with her for one week. After that first week, we met as a group with manager Mr. M at a restaurant and exchanged tips, stories, and information. We also got a chance to visit local churches to seek out hosts.

That Sunday I visited a Baptist church, stated my predicament to someone in charge and was directed to a woman willing to accommodate me for a few weeks. Her name was Geraldine. There was an overweight man living with her, who did not speak to me and who seemed very ill. He spent a lot of time in bed. She also had a teenage daughter. I worked six days a week, twelve hours a day door-to-door, so I was unable to spend any time with my "hosts." I basically just ate a little dinner and slept there. I helped out by cleaning the kitchen at night and offering Geraldine money for food. After I had exhausted all the neighborhoods within walking distance of Geraldine's house, I needed to seek out a new territory in Houston. She recommended a man to me by the name of Dallas—an understandable name for someone living in Texas.

Dallas was a veteran of some war who used a prosthesis for one leg. Jenny needed a new place to stay as well, so Dallas agreed to let Jenny and me use his house during our last month in Houston. In terms of sleeping arrangements, he offered us a choice between the floor in an unfurnished bedroom or his comfortable king-size bed, which we would have to share with him. We took the cold floor, making it comfortable enough with blankets and pillows.

After that first night, Dallas was not home the entire time we used his house, which was about four weeks. We each had a house key, free use of the kitchen and bathroom, and kept our sleeping quarters in the unfurnished bedroom. I don't recall his asking for money, but it was our policy to share a small portion of our earnings with our hosts. I didn't appreciate his kindness then as much as I do now. I guess I was too cautious at the time.

Jenny and I claimed different areas of the surrounding neighborhood so that we would not overlap each other's territories. After we covered every home in each of our territories, we purchased used bikes and rode to more distant areas. We must have been a strange sight to motorists. Here were two determined young women, riding old rickety bikes on major roadways along with massive tractor trailers and speeding cars. Jenny went her own way after about two weeks. She found a place to stay in a richer neighborhood, I think. I stayed at Dallas' place for the remaining few weeks.

In addition to my gracious hosts, I met some other very memorable people who showed me kindness. As I stopped at one middle-class home, a gentle, soft-spoken man who I think was both a husband and father pointed out that there was something wrong with my bike. He then proceeded to fix it for me without charging me anything. I had no idea that anything was amiss. That man's action really touched me. Several people bought my books just to help me out. One guy who was on military leave made me a peanut butter and jelly sandwich then asked me out on a date. I could not accept since I was bone tired after I stopped work at seven. Another listened as I told him about the Lord and then he bought a Bible. I will always remember those kind people who met my needs while I was in Houston.

All of my experiences in Houston were not so positive. There was one neighborhood that brought me to tears. It wasn't run-down, poverty-stricken or filled with sad sights of neglected children. The homes in this neighborhood were new and beautiful with wood stained doors, lots of gables, flawless siding and flowering shrubs. The lawns were landscaped professionally. The sidewalks were clean and smooth as if fresh concrete had been recently poured. There was no litter in the street, or one stray weed growing. I was at first pleased that the few owners I met were African-American. I had never seen African Americans live so well collectively; everything was immaculate on the outside—but something was amiss. It was high noon in the good ole summertime and not one child was outside playing. Every single window on ground level and every single door had security bars obscuring the craftsmanship. Not one window was open. No bird sang. It was like a ghost town.

I went from door to door, ringing bells and knocking, without any response for about five hours, from seven in the morning until noon. Exhausted from the heat and lack of food and water, my upbeat salesman-like attitude plummeted. During the summer that Houston was experiencing a drought, I was walking about in a treeless neighborhood without water, food or a refuge from the scorching sun. The people here had desirable homes, but I would not want to live in any of them. The fear with which these residents lived was palpable and oppressive. They were prisoners in their own homes. By the time someone finally answered the doorbell, I was emotionally and physically drained.

The owner spoke to me through a tiny peephole in the door, which was reinforced with iron security bars. Even after she slid open the slot in the door's decorative window, which was probably made with bulletproof glass, we were still separated by a heavy dose of fear. No matter how much charm I mustered, she would not open the door. She would not hear my sales pitch. My emotions overwhelmed me and I started to sob, asking the lady on the other side of the barrier, "Why is your neighborhood like this?" She muttered something and slammed the slot closed. I mechanically moved on to the next house thinking that I really needed to leave this place.

A few houses later I got another response. A man of obvious leisure, well-dressed in his pajamas, answered the doorbell, swinging the door open wide. Well, I thought to myself, *Finally!* He looked pleased to see me and when I came to the part of the sales pitch where I ask to come in, he motioned for me to enter his home with a smile on his face. It was such a relief to finally get inside a cool air-conditioned home and to sit down after walking for over five hours in the hot, summer Texas sun. He was in the middle of preparing himself a fabulous brunch and offered me a plate of food which I could in no wise resist. I hungrily gobbled down the scrambled eggs, bacon, toast and orange juice. I immediately perked up.

After thanking him for the meal, I proceeded to give him the rest of the sales pitch. He was not interested in my books; instead he interrupted my presentation, offering me some recreational fun in his bedroom. I decided that there was no use trying to sell this person any of my products, and while he may have needed the Lord, I was not the person for that job either. I packed up my sales kit, thanked him for the food, and made a quick exit. I had enough of that neighborhood.

The job as a door-to-door salesperson definitely had a down side. Most of the time, I was at the mercy of strangers and quite vulnerable. However, I learned to trust God for safety and provisions and after that last neighborhood I made it a habit to pray more as I walked about alone in Houston.

I did have a few opportunities to share my faith. I met a Jewish woman who was married to an African American man who did not treat her well. As we sat on the couch in her home, she cried and told me about her sad, disappointing marriage. I told her that Jesus was Jewish and that he loved her and that he was the Messiah. I showed her some scriptures. She seemed encouraged, dried her eyes and bought a Bible. After leaving her, I walked through a very poor area that resembled some type of slave quarters. It had a row of one-room wooden shacks with peeling paint strung out along a dirt road. I gave my sales presentation to one tenant—a young, handsome, muscular man with skin the color of walnut wood—living in one of the closet-like dwellings. The room was barely big enough to accommodate a twin bed and a chair. I did not notice an adjacent bathroom or kitchen. Maybe there was a community building that housed these facilities. As he sat on the bed and I on the chair, he listened intently as I gave him my sales pitch and then explained a few scriptures to him. He ordered a Bible. I wish now that I had the foresight to follow up with these two precious people once I returned home.

The last week was set aside to deliver the ordered books to my customers. That meant I needed a car. Our supervisor advised us to start seeking early for that car by asking folks in the churches, our hosts, and our customers. Shortly before that last week, I was giving my sales pitch to a rugged African American man I'll call Sly who painted for a living. He seemed to be in his late forties, was slim and smelled slightly of alcohol. He appeared to live alone and spoke nothing of a family. He seemed to think I was amusing, grinning and chuckling as I went through my lines. He put down the deposit for a Bible and I was emboldened. As I finished the paperwork for the sale, I asked if he knew of anyone who could loan me a car to deliver books for a week. He sat up straight and quickly offered his. He was true to his word. When it was time to deliver the goods, Sly gave me the keys to his car.

Things got a little tricky along the way. He accompanied me as I drove his car to the homes of my customers, and after a few days he insisted that I pay for his services by being intimate with him. I told him that I was waiting for marriage and he did not believe me. During several more delivery trips, he nagged constantly about my refusing his request, but by remaining extremely busy and focusing on my work, I managed to avoid being alone with him.

His car took a toll. After using it for five days to deliver all of my customers' orders, it broke down. I had to take Sly's word for it because it was still working the last time I drove it. I felt bad about his car but concentrated my efforts on getting back to New York.

On the last night at Dallas's house, I packed up my things. Jenny came and joined me for we planned to meet Tina the next day for our trip home. I was prepared to say a speedy farewell to Sly over the phone and go to bed early. He had other plans. I was surprised to see his car pull up in front of Dallas's house that balmy evening in August. I met him in the driveway hoping that the visit would be short. He walked towards me and said, "Don't leave me this way," and then he pulled me close and kissed me. I could smell cigarettes and alcohol as he pressed himself hard against me, but it was an effective kiss. I started to melt in his arms…wanting to give in…then quickly came to my senses. I tensed up and pushed him away. I had to escape. This was not in my plan. I quickly explained to him that I appreciate what he had done for me but I had to leave the next day. I told him also that I was tired and needed to get some sleep and then said goodnight. He followed me into the kitchen and asked for a drink. I served him some juice, said good-bye again and went into the empty bedroom. After exchanging a few words with Jenny, I made up my spot on the floor, closed the bedroom door and she and I laid our heads on our pillows ready to dream about going home. We were exhausted from our summer job. We had done it. We had completed our tough assignment in Texas and were wiped out. I couldn't worry about Sly. I just knew he would understand and go on home. I quickly fell asleep.

In the morning, I got up to scramble some eggs. I didn't have to sell or deliver books but could finally relax and eat a good breakfast. Jenny was packing her last-minute items and then left the house to run some last-minute errand. Soon, we would meet up with Tina and then be on our way home. I was in for a surprise when I entered the kitchen. Sly was sitting on the living room sofa with a smirk on his face. He slept on the couch and was a little more than annoyed. He said he waited up all night expecting me to join him in the living room sometime during the night after Jenny fell asleep. It sounded very enticing; still I was shocked that we were worlds apart in our thinking. I thought his "don't leave me this way" meant something else, such as don't leave me with a broken heart. I told him that I was sorry that he had expected what he did and that I honestly did not know that he was waiting for me. In fact, I was secretly glad that I didn't know, realizing that I may not have been able to resist the temptation after that kiss and all he had done for me. He knew I had to go back to college so he let his frustrations go, insisting instead that we write and call each other. I agreed to stay in touch.

I packed up and hurried off with Jenny to meet with Tina. The three of us were all greatly relieved to be leaving our summer in Houston behind. We stopped in Nashville to drop off the company's sales kit and to pick up our paycheck. My pay after expenses was $2,000. Between the three of us, I made the least amount of money, but that was the biggest check I'd ever earned so it was adequate compensation for me.

After leaving Nashville, as I was driving Tina's borrowed Volkswagen Rabbit along the interstate highway, I felt tremendous heat on the floor of the car and from the dashboard. The oil light was on. Tina said the light was broken, so we ignored the light and continued on. As the miles increased on the odometer so did the heat from the engine. It was uncomfortably hot behind the wheel but I kept on driving. Finally, the engine started knocking and I was forced to pull over on a rural highway in pitch blackness somewhere between Tennessee and Arkansas. We turned on the hazard lights and inched along until we spotted an isolated car repair garage that seemed to appear out of nowhere. We stopped and explained our problem to the men working at the place. There in front of our eyes, three or four mechanics proceeded to take the Rabbit completely apart and build it into a different vehicle from the chassis up. We left the old engine behind and pulled out with a vehicle that felt like a hyped-up go-cart. By God's grace, we made it home to New York in that shaky, rattling re-constructed marvel. After Tina presented the car to her relatives in Long Island it was soon banished to the junk yard.

It took Tina and me some time to get over our adventure. Our nerves were a bit frazzled, but our friendship was refined like gold in the fire. I never heard from Jenny again, but Tina and I remained close friends until she moved away with her new husband to Illinois almost ten years later. Thereafter we kept in touch with Christmas cards.

During that summer in Texas, I learned to appreciate Tina's bold, independent spirit. If it were not for her courage to take on such a job, I would have missed out on the thrill of living like a nomad on the edge and putting my life completely in God's hands. I also learned to appreciate the Carpenters. We only had one good audio cassette to listen to as we traveled hundred of miles on the highway, and we played that Carpenters tape over and over again. What a beautiful voice and unique singing style Karen Carpenter had.

Safely back in my dormitory, I called Sly on the hallway pay phone and left him a message. He called me back and confessed that he had taken fifty dollars from my money envelope to compensate himself for the loss of his car. I should have offered him more money than I did. I was too immature to do the right thing so I felt he deserved to help himself to some of the cash. I was also glad about the distance between us.

Over the next few weeks he continued to call insisting first that I visit him in December, then that I move permanently to Houston and then that I marry him. After a few letters and a few more phone calls, he gave up on me, angrily calling me a whore. I never meant to hurt him.

Dad and I probably could have spent hours trading stories—my adventures in Houston and his in Korea. How meaningful that time would have been to me.

I know I would have marveled at some of the things Dad experienced and he could have given me a good dose of common sense. I was naïve, but Jesus was faithful to protect one of his most simple-hearted followers.

When Mr. M came around in the spring to recruit us for the following summer, Tina and I were ready with our answer, which was a positive and definite "No." The first time I accepted the job ignorantly. I could not commit myself again knowing the temptations and dangers ahead. Nothing Mr. M said could make Tina and me change our minds. As his eyes narrowed with an icy coldness after we gave our final answer, we knew we had made the right decision.

Chapter 17

A Flame Dies; a Light Dawns

"I lie in the dust, completely discouraged; revive me by your word."
Psalm 119:25 (NLT)

After exposure to a full day of sun for ten weeks in Houston, my facial skin was beyond a shade or two darker. It was dehydrated and sunburnt. I did wear a cotton visor to shield my eyes, but it did little to protect my hair and the rest of my face from the sun's potent rays. With a dried-out complexion and hair as brittle as straw, I had turned into part scarecrow.

Mom told me that during the summer Walter called. That information was heard, quickly processed then dismissed to the inactive files in my head. I never expected Dad to contact me. He was living his life. I was living mine. But Bounce had agreed to visit me.

I finally got a call from him, and our first conversation after years of being apart was not as wonderful as I had hoped. He said that he was "not in love with me, that he's not changing for me, that he has gotta be himself...that he still does things." He wanted me because he needs "someone righteous." His feelings for me "will grow into love." Right now he just cared and that I "should not put anyone down because they're not Christian enough." He asked me if I was still a virgin and was glad to hear that I was. He said he would call again and that from my picture he could see that I was "looking better and finally learned to dress."

So my plan had worked. All of my begging and pleading with God had pulled Bounce right back to me. I wasn't so excited though for two reasons. First he admitted that he did not love me. Well, I was looking for love and could not accept anything less. Secondly, the timing was off. He was planning to visit me way too soon—right after my summer in Houston—before the damage from the sun was repaired—before I was ready—before I felt attractive.

A few weeks after the first call, he phoned again and said he could come over right away. I panicked knowing that I still needed a couple of months of beauty recovery treatments. My skin needed to rejuvenate and my hair needed more intense treatments (I was introduced to hair conditioners). I should have told him to come back next year—I mean I waited all this time—another year would not hurt—but I said okay. This was definitely not the way I envisioned our reunion. I was actually dreading it.

Within hours, there was a knock at the door. I wanted someone else, like Mom, to open it and say that I had run out on an urgent call. Yet, I had earnestly desired this moment, had prayed fervently for it and now I needed to gather up the courage to face him.

I opened the door. There standing before me, filling in the door frame was a rough-looking, darkened man, with hardened features, towering six feet or more, who I did not know nor cared to know. This was definitely not the youthful boy I remembered. How could five years make such a difference? Where was the smooth-skinned, bouncy teenager about my height, with the gleam in his eyes that I once knew?

I could tell that this stranger was just as repulsed by me by the look in his eyes. I wanted to shut the door; he probably wanted to turn and run. Out of sheer politeness I invited him in. He hesitated and then reluctantly walked through the kitchen and into the living room. We sat down stiffly on the couch at a safe distance from each other. There was a quick, awkward exchange of words. I was relieved when he left. My infatuation with Bounce was over.

I remembered the dreams and confessed, "Lord Jesus... You were right. Bounce is not the one for me. I should have listened to you in the first place. The person I loved doesn't even exist, but was someone I had dreamed up in my tainted imagination." I thought I had it all figured out and could solve my own problems, but this entire obsession with Bounce was an exercise in self-delusion. I surrendered the responsibility of my love life to Someone who could handle it.

The last bit of news I heard about Bounce was dreadfully chilling. Several years later, I was stunned to find out that he was no more, killed by a bullet in the street. I was saddened. I knew him when he was full of promise.

* * *

My senior year at King's was lonely and depressing. I was discouraged most of the time, but kept my thoughts to myself. I could not even manage to get a date with anyone. There were few African American men on campus and all of the ones interested in dating were spoken for. Besides the void in my love life, I was confused about what I would do with my life once I graduated. I had decided to become a teacher too late. In order to complete the requirements for certification, I would have to attend college for an additional year. I didn't want to burden my mom with any more school expenses. I chose to major in religious education, which I could finish within the normal four years. To this day, I realize that I should have extended my education another two semesters to secure my certification requirements. Instead, I graduated from King's in May of 1981 with a liberal arts degree. My mom and an aunt were there standing in the crowd waiting for me, very proud and happy. I didn't feel that there was that much to celebrate. I had a degree but no career. I was not going to be a teacher or a nurse. I had to accept whatever employment I could find.

When I got home that summer, I was in for a little surprise. Mom had moved again! A fire (suspected work of an arsonist) in the old apartment building caused enough smoke and water damage that she could not continue to live there. She accepted temporary shelter two blocks away in an eighty-year-old colonial of a coworker at the hospital. This single, kind-hearted man offered her three bedrooms, one for herself and two others for her children, Neil and me. I moved my belongings from college into a furnished bedroom on the second floor. It was nice to finally have my own room. Valerie was living away from home.

That summer I sought employment that interested me and learned how much fun little boys were. I was hired as a camp counselor at a Salvation Army sleep-away camp. My first assignment was to supervise eight nine-year-old girls and I had a miserable time. I could do little to make their time at camp enjoyable. Some of the assertive ones voiced their dislike of the food, the cabins, the spiders, the outdoor activities and each other. That was pretty much everything. Their negative attitudes spoiled the possibility of fun for the entire group. I spent most of my time putting out the fires of complaints and dissension. I did not want to repeat this experience for another six weeks, and

I thought about quitting but settled on hoping that the next group would be easier.

Then I was told that my assignment for the next session was to watch over eight nine-year-old boys. I panicked. What was I going to do with eight boys! They would devour me! I'd end up running for my life through the woods somewhere. I pictured eight selfish, egotistical, rock-throwing, stick-swinging, cursing, spitting, aggressive little men, all foiling the feeble attempts of their timid and inexperienced counselor to lead them through an enjoyable two-week camp experience. However, two years on the high school track team trained me to not quit. I had to do something, so I prayed for help. Over the next six weeks, I led three sessions of campers, all boys, and to my surprise, I enjoyed it immensely.

I connected really well with the boys; they were easy-going, fun, appreciative and totally refreshing. They loved the food, hungrily cleaning their plates and going back for seconds and thirds! They sang and marched to the clever, military-style camp songs. Spiders and bugs were appreciated! I could make them happy with sticks and strings as we pretended to go fishing in the little dirty pond. Although they were all different (chubby, thin, African American, Hispanic, and white, quiet and rambunctious) they respected one another. My last group got along so well that we were able to put on a short skit on the final night which involved three of my campers impersonating characters of their choice: Fred Sanford, the Incredible Hulk and a street pimp.

After camp ended, I received a few tender letters complete with photos from some of the boys. I wrote back and even visited one in his parents' New York City apartment. I absolutely loved the job but had to move on. The work was seasonal and the pay was too low, but I was glad to have had this valuable experience which evaporated all of my preconceived notions about a particular group of little people.

* * *

Mom informed me that Walter called again while I was at camp during the summer. The information was acknowledged and discarded.

In the fall I joined a temporary employment agency. My first long-term assignment was at IBM, the company which eventually hired me permanently as a secretary. It wasn't what I loved to do, such as working with children, but it offered a good salary, benefits and opportunities for advancement.

One Saturday, I was in Mom's bedroom looking out of her bay window to the street below. It was a dreary day and I had nothing to do. My mother's phone rang and I picked it up. It was a male voice.

He said, "Hi, Felicia! How are you doing!?!"

I had no idea who the caller was. My first impression was that he was a telemarketer who got my name off some list, but he didn't launch into a sales pitch.

"Who is this?" I asked, dumbfounded. I could not place the voice. It was so unlike me to forget someone who I was supposed to remember. I prided myself on thinking of every individual in my life enough to remember at least the circumstances in which we met, if not his or her name. The upbeat voice continued.

"I've finally reached you! You are soooooo hard to catch up with! How have you beeeeeeen!!??"

"Okay, thanks, but who is this??" I questioned, trying hard to identify this confident, upbeat person that I had forgotten.

"You don't know? Guess!!" said Mr. Playful.

"Uhhh…uh…I am…not sure…talk some more," was the best I could do as I racked my brain.

"What??? You don't know who I am??? You've forgotten me…already???? My feelings are really hurt!" whined the voice, feigning rejection.

This person had time for games and I didn't. I needed to get back to looking out the window. I chuckled impatiently at his teasing. I was too baffled to enjoy the humor. I could not, to save my life, identify the owner of this voice. He on the other hand was having a grand time as cheerful teasing oozed out between each word. He continued his phony lamenting.

"How could you have forgotten me? I didn't forget you. How could you forget such a wonderful, handsome guy as me! You've hurt me deep down within, Felicia. I am wounded to the core."

"I am sorry but I just don't remember. Am I supposed to know you?"

"Of course!!! None of the girls forget me!" he boasted in a high-pitched tone and then he laughed.

That was the trigger. If I remembered nothing else, I remembered the laugh. At the sound of that laugh, my brain's memory neurons fell into place and connected to…a time, a place, a face and a name.

"Oh, you're Walter Johnson from Colgate," I exclaimed, immensely relieved that my brain was working again.

He laughed again. "Yeah, you got it!!!"

Now that the mystery caller was solved, I was perplexed. Why he was calling me? We had no connection other than a short-term, meaningless acquaintance.

"I'm glad you finally remembered me."

"Oh, yeah…well, uh…I never expected you to call. Why are you calling?" I said, at the risk of sounding rude.

"I was just going through the Colgate directory and I saw your name there and was wondering how you were doing, so I figured I'd give my old friend a call. There's no harm in that, is there?"

I didn't realize we were friends but didn't argue the point. I could use a friend.

After catching up with a few details and sharing some memories about Colgate, we decided to try to get together to go to the zoo. I learned that he didn't have a car and would have to take a bus, then a train, then a taxi to come to see me from his home in Bergen County, New Jersey. I didn't want him going through all that trouble just to see me. So I told him that we should wait until he got a car.

I guess I did not explain myself too well, because again I offended him. He thought I was arrogantly demanding that he have a vehicle before he even thought about seeing me since I expected to be chauffeured. I didn't mean it that way and didn't hear from him until the following year. He had purchased his car: a brand-new 1982 burnt orange, four-door Toyota Tercel.

He called because he was simply looking for a good friend. He already had a girlfriend who lived in Vienna, Virginia, but he made it his practice to maintain as many male and female friends locally as possible. He said he found me delightful and fun to talk with so he decided that I would be one of his local friends.

He began calling on a weekly basis because this method worked when someone befriended him. I got the hang of it and began calling him as well and soon I invited him over. I didn't expect him to come though he said he would. I was accustomed to men who made empty promises, and I didn't think he'd be any different.

Instead, he surprised me. He arrived at two o'clock promptly on a Sunday afternoon, a most inconvenient time for me because I had a church service at 4:00. He stayed about an hour, during which I served him a dinner of green peppers stuffed with rice and hamburger, and then I had to rush back to church to sing in the afternoon program. He left graciously with a pleasant attitude and a smile.

I didn't think of him as my "Mr. Right" or "Mr. Possibility." I reasoned, if we were supposed to be together, why didn't sparks fly when we were at Colgate? He also didn't fit into my preconceptions of what my "Mr. Right" would look and act like, so I hatched a plan to scare him off.

During our next conversation, I hit him with my best weapon that killed every other prospect.

"If we are going to spend time together, I would like for us to read the Bible and go to church together."

The next time Walter came over, he enthusiastically brought his Bible with him. Then we went to church. This was going to be harder to shake than I thought.

He continued to befriend, calling and inviting me out on little day trips with him. Walter was an outdoor guy. He took me for walks in beautiful parks and boating out on lakes. One of his favorite spots was the Delaware Water Gap, where we'd go for picnics. He also took me out to dinner at fancy restaurants, an experience that was very new to me. I'd invite him to church and roller-skating. As we spent time together, I began to thoroughly enjoy his platonic friendship and I began to see how much we had in common. As a matter of fact, I started to love spending innocent and uncomplicated time with him.

One of our earliest dates in a park on the Palisades in New Jersey.

It was nice to have someone with whom I could converse at length and in depth. We talked about his girlfriends, the men in my life, the church, our families, our jobs, and anything that popped into my head. Much of the time, I would talk and he would listen.

He was a manager at a CVS drug store during this time and always had to work Saturday or Sundays. I coveted his time so much that I forced him to agree that the next time he had a two- or three-day break in his schedule we would spend a whole day together instead of just a few hours. When that time arrived, he instead went down to Virginia to see his girlfriend without even telling me. I was expecting him to spend at least one of his three vacation days with me, and he wasted all of them on that woman. I promptly wrote him a letter and mailed it, letting him know that I was hurt when he did not spend the day with me as he promised. I had no idea that while he was in Virginia, he and his girlfriend broke up. He read more into my letter than I meant to convey. He felt that I missed him, which was true, but he also thought that I had developed a romantic interest in him. I simply was sincerely thrilled to have a true friend of the opposite sex for the first time in my life.

There was another time when I sent the wrong message. We went roller-skating at Skate Key in the Bronx. After skating together for several songs, we decided to rest. (I probably did not like the song that was playing.) Feeling a real close bond growing between us, I expressed my appreciation for his friendship by resting my head on his shoulders. He thought I was sending a romantic message, but I was just thankful to have the simple, true, unconditional, innocent love of this man at my side. It nourished me.

About the same time that Walter broke up with his girlfriend, I stopped spending time with someone with whom I obviously had no future. I told Walter about the situation, who by that time secretly wanted to be next in line. When a charming guy from the West Indies started showing interest, Walter told me later that he was so upset he didn't want to speak to anyone that day. I thought this guy from Grenada was God's choice for me. He was an acquaintance in high school and I met up with him again by chance as we were walking down the same street. On our first date, we went to a park and under a beautiful summer's moon and he shared his testimony of how God had worked in his life. I was impressed by his faith in God. In addition, he was dark skinned, refined and handsome enough, and I felt that I was falling in love. A week later, after attending a banquet dinner at a hotel with him that honored my pastor, he cornered me in the hotel elevator and lifted up my blouse. That move ended my infatuation with him. I told Walter about it as soon as I could the next day. All he said was "don't think about it." I felt slighted by his indifference. I thought he cared more. I learned later that he was overjoyed that this guy had committed the unpardonable and was now history.

We were both suddenly free, without romantic attachments. Walter began to send out gentle signals that any other woman would have been glad to answer. When we took walks in his neighborhood, he tried to hold my hand. I ran ahead. When he looked deep into my eyes, I avoided his. Our friendship was so cozy and comfortable I didn't want it to change.

I, who have been looking for love all of my life, couldn't understand why I was rejecting romance with such a nice person. Typically I would have welcomed such attention from a man. I finally admitted to myself that I was still looking for someone like Dad with a super-big ego to compensate for my lack thereof; Walter failed there. I just did not want him to look like Dad or be light skinned; Walter failed there. I was trapped in a pattern of being attracted to the wrong guy and at the same time trying to avoid him. I asked the Lord to help me because I was too mixed up to trust or even know my own heart.

I heard that God wants us to be specific when we pray, so I developed a list of what I wanted in a man. I put it in the form of a poem so I could recall it when I needed to check off my list.

A tall, a six-footer, well-roasted by the sun,
With legs of iron and arms well-built,
Who loves to have some fun,
In tickling, laughing, and all kinds of games,
Basketball, bicycling, skating and things.
A lover of God, he must also be,
Able to read the Bible with me.

The toughest requirement I had was not expressed explicitly in that poem. The man for me would have to be able to wait until marriage for sexual intimacy. If I wanted God's best, I would have to do things God's way. It even made sense to wait because that decision alone tested and eliminated many with wicked intentions.

Walter and I continued on as friends for a more than a year. Then the owner of the house I lived in, Mr. Ward, intervened. He was tired of watching my slow progress as Walter hung on. One day in 1984, Mr. Ward approached me.

"When are you going to make a move on Walter? He likes you. You can't keep having him come see you without doing something about it."

I wondered what Mr. Ward was talking about.

"Oh, we're just friends, Mr. Ward. He has lots of female friends he visits and I am just one of them," I replied, wishing he'd drop the subject. I wanted to continue to "play" with my friend without growing up.

However, he went on.

"No man is going to spend time and money on a woman if he doesn't like her. I'm telling you he wants more out of this thing. I've seen the look in his eye and how he comes over through all sorts of weather, rain, snowstorms and blizzards at your beck and call. You can't do this to a man. You shouldn't have him coming over here all the time if you don't want him. If you're not interested, you gotta let him know."

Oh, he was treading on sensitive ground. He was asking me to be responsible. I just wanted to be "Walter's little girl."

"But you don't know Walter like I do. You haven't seen him at college. He was always walking the campus visiting his female friends all the time, without any strings attached," I argued. I wanted this beautiful simplistic relationship to go on that way forever. If we complicated it with romance it might fall apart. Mr. Ward continued pressing his point.

"Walter is no fool. He's not gonna hang around forever! You have got to make a move...or he'll soon be gone and you'll miss your chance!"

"But we are fine just as friends. He hasn't said anything to me about changing the relationship."

"I'm telling you! You can't use a man like this. You've got to make a choice, Felicia. Let him go if you don't want him."

Then he added, "He's the one for you! If you don't make a move soon, I will!"

I was planning on ignoring the whole situation, now he was forcing my hand. I continued to protest.

"He is just a friend. He doesn't like me that way!"

Mr. Ward simply repeated his threat.

"I told you Walter is no fool. He wouldn't be doing all this for nothing. I see the way he looks at you and dresses up when he comes over...in his suit and all. I've seen the look in his eyes. You can't keep using a man like that. If you don't make a move, I'm gonna tell Walter to stop coming over, 'cause you're not interested!"

I decided to confront Walter myself to prove Mr. Ward wrong. Walter could speak for himself. He didn't need Mr. Ward to do it for him.

The next time Walter came over, we sat on the living room sofa to spend time talking. I brought up the subject I had tried to avoid.

"Walter, I need to talk to you about something."

"Okay," he nodded.

"I need to know...well, Mr. Ward says...that you are attracted to me. I told him we were just friends, but he didn't believe me...I...I guess I need to hear what you say."

After a moment of silence, he said, "Well...Felicia...to be honest...I have been attracted to you...for some time, now."

At the same time, I was pleased and disappointed. I knew he had been trying to reach out to me romantically, but because I was not ready I chose to ignore him. Now, the party was over. I had to make a choice. On the other hand, I was pleased that I had won his affection.

The man I tried to run from. We stopped to enjoy the scenery along a country road while visiting Grandmother Fields in 1984.

Walter was such wonderful friend to me that I simply couldn't let him fade away. Though I was not "in love" like in the movies, he had won me over by freely giving his friendship without expecting anything in return. I repressed my doubts and questions and decided to give love a chance. I thought a slow dance would be a good way to start our new relationship.

I picked up a long-playing album by the Gospel Keynotes and played their song "God's Love Is Real." When Walter wrapped his arms around me and gently kissed my forehead, I melted. I felt heaven open and all the hugs that God had for me pouring down through this man. I felt the Lord confirming what Mr. Ward had said, "He is the one for you." What a surprise! The Lord definitely stretched my thinking for I would have never picked Walter for myself.

After our relationship got serious, I learned quickly to call Walter by his middle name, Irvin, since whenever I called his home and asked for "Walter," his father came to the phone.

The next day on October 31, 1983, I sent him this letter:

Dear Irvin:

I just had to write you this letter—to jot down some of my thoughts—maybe it will help me to clear my head... I know I send you mixed, confused messages sometimes; that's because I'm undecided or rather unsure about my heart's desires. You said last night that you didn't want to complicate my life, but I'm so glad you did... I'm glad you didn't give up on me. Last night I could hardly sleep. I tossed and turned all night long... went to bed with you on my mind and woke up with you in my thoughts... when you danced with me. I didn't know a girl could feel so good. I was so touched and so astounded; I was so moved and felt so loved that I cried after you left... I see that you're a wonderful, marvelous mature man... even now when I listen to the song we danced to, I cry... Last night was real. I feel the same way toward you that I felt towards Edrich only a week ago... I'll be your girlfriend... give me a little time before we declare ourselves as going steady... but for now consider us romantically involved... "

I received Walter's letter a few weeks later.

11/12/83

My Dearest Felicia,

Words when they come from the heart be they written or spoken are like music. Your last letter is a song that has warmed my heart. Truthful and honest, sweet and sincere. Even if we never go beyond a good friendship, you, I will always treasure and memories have already been made that I'll never forget. One day at a time is often the best way to do things. Recently I have found myself praying not only for you but for us. That God willing, in time, we will come together. There are a lot of reasons why I could say I'm attracted to you but the greatest reason of all is not very easy to explain. The best way I can describe it to you is to say that sometimes it just feels so right. Oh, but one day at a time ... I hope you never lose the faith you have. I have always had the greatest admiration for it. I see you as a woman who is small in stature but yet very strong ...

Love always, Irv

Courtship was a dizzying roller coaster ride for both of us. Some days I felt like I loved him. Some days I didn't like him at all as my old patterns of thinking surfaced. On those days I didn't even like myself and I thought there was something wrong with him because he thought I was adorable. He endured my skittishness as I sought for confirmations from the Lord, my family, friends and church constantly because I was not always sure if we were supposed to be together. Some days he'd call, saying "I love you" and I'd snap, "What is love!" He'd answer that love is a decision. He was a rock. While my emotions were up and down, Irvin was steadfast and true. Before Irvin came into my life, I thought I was a stable and well-balanced person. Now I knew better. I was my father's daughter and though I seemed well-adjusted on the outside, there was confusing murkiness under the paint. My hidden insecurities did not allow for a very romantic beginning, but when you start at the dusty bottom, with God's grace, it only gets better.

Chapter 18

Pain Revealed

"A motive in the human heart is like deep water, and a person who has understanding draws it out."
Proverbs 20:5 (GOD'S WORD)

Mom was granted her divorce that following summer of 1982 after living apart from Dad for eight years. Although the court years ago sided with Dad, the divorce papers were drawn up by African American lawyers who heard Mom's side of the story. The papers said that Dad, the defendant,

"...has been guilty of cruel and inhuman treatment towards the plaintiff in that the defendant has caused the plaintiff to suffer grievous anguish and anxiety so as to make it mentally and physically unsafe for her to cohabit with the defendant... The defendant did commence upon a course of conduct wherein he did abuse the plaintiff in that he treated her in a cruel and inhuman manner.

"The constructive abandonment of the plaintiff by the defendant was without justification."

Mom was free to restart her life. She enjoyed a budding romance with Mr. Ward, while my relationship with Irvin was sifting me like wheat. As Irvin and I spent time together, issues that lurked deep within me rose to the surface. He wanted to enlarge our social circle to include his group of friends. If I had a healthy level of self-esteem, that would not have been a problem, but I was a person who took comfort in hiding. Irvin wanted to present me to the world.

I hated the pressure of being Irvin's girlfriend. Irrational fear came upon me when he tried to take me to parties. Once, we traveled all the way to the door of an apartment in the Bronx and I did not let him knock on it. I was much too insecure to enter that place full of strangers, all of whom were most likely expecting a fashionably dressed, self-assured, educated woman at their friend's side who could hold a conversation. I worried that I would be the object of subtle rejection. Irvin reassured me that all would be fine, that his friends were very nice people and finally, after feeling very foolish, I allowed him to knock on the door. I sheepishly followed him into the crowded apartment, cowering inside my skin. We sat down on a couch. Soon Irvin got up and mingled as other guests engaged in relaxed talk holding drinks in one hand and gesturing or eating with the other. For the most part, I was ignored, thankfully. Knowing that I was not having a good time, Irvin took me home long before the party ended.

Another time, after Irvin was hired by an insurance company, he and other new hires were roomed together in a Manhattan apartment at the company's expense while they completed a two-day training session. When he was ready to go home, I offered to give him a ride home in my speedy little Honda Civic hatchback. I knocked on the door of the apartment; he opened it, greeted me and invited me in, but I preferred to wait at the door. He went back into the apartment to bring the other trainees to the door to introduce me, but when he came back I was nowhere in sight. I had run off to stand by the elevator. Irvin told his coworkers, "I don't know where she went. She was here a minute ago!"

One evening a few months later, Irvin asked me to attend a church service. He was selling insurance by then and one of his female clients invited him to a concert in which she was singing over in Hackensack, New Jersey. He drove over to Mount Vernon to pick me up. I said I would go, but I was afraid to. When a man walks around with a woman on his arms everyone evaluates her to see if she is physically worthy. I felt that the scrutiny would again lead to rejection and just did not want to face it. Irvin was perplexed and wanted to know why I refused to go with him. We sat down on the couch. I knew that I needed to verbalize to him what I was feeling because he was so confused by my behavior.

"Well, I don't want to embarrass you."

"Embarrass me…you won't embarrass me. Why do you say that?"

"Well, I just…I just don't want to feel rejected."

"Rejected? Why would you think you would be rejected?"

"Well, because…well I guess I just feel…uh, sometimes I can see it in people's eyes and sometimes I just feel too ugly."

"Ugly? Why do you feel ugly?"

I always thought that God gave Irvin strange and unusual vision. He thought I was attractive and wanted to show me off. I didn't understand what he saw, was relieved that he was pleased with me, but sometimes I thought that he was partially deranged.

Irvin was still waiting for an answer and wanting to understand. He repeated himself.

"I don't understand. Why do you feel that you are ugly?"

"Because I am…that's what people say. I have always been ugly."

"I don't know why you say that. You are not ugly."

No matter what Irvin said, I was not convinced by his words. I just could not bring myself to believe that I was anywhere near what he thought I was. I dug deeper to determine why I felt so strongly about my own repulsiveness.

"Well…the kids in school used to call me names like 'four-eyes,' 'monkey-ears,' ugly…"

"Felicia, you are not ugly. You are beautiful to me," he insisted with a sincere, urgent voice.

I could feel his sincerity as I stared down into my lap. I was encouraged by his patience and his assessment, but I still felt despicable deep down within. So I thought harder to find why I could not simply accept his words. He looked intently at me, silently expecting a reasonable explanation. I tried to verbalize my deep feelings again.

"Well…it's just something I have always been; people have always called me ugly. My first boyfriend said I was ugly. I never knew how to dress, or fix up my hair, and I have to wear these stupid glasses…"

"But, you're not ugly."

"Well…I feel that I am."

"Why do you keep saying that? I think you are very pretty. I don't understand why you feel that way. One of the prettiest things about you is that you don't know that you're attractive and so you're not arrogant about it."

I was silent, thinking of the answers to his "whys." He continued.

"I just don't understand why you think you are ugly," he said as he shook his head in wonder.

He really cared. He really wanted to solve this issue. So I continued searching for reasons, thinking back in time, trying to trace back to when I first knew that I was ugly.

I poured out some more words.

"I've always felt this way…since I was little. My dad… My dad…" My voice broke off. Tears welled up in my eyes. I had found the source and the buried wound. It opened and pain gushed up from inside and burst out in the form of hot, salty tears.

"My Dad…called me…funny-looking…" I sobbed uncontrollably.

That was it. That was the source of my self-loathing and insecurity. Daddy, who I had dismissed from my life, was as real and powerful to me at that moment as when he stood in the kitchen and said those words to me so long ago. I was that little five-year-old girl again, and all the pain I buried then hit me in this moment. Only this time it was safe to cry.

I covered my face with my hands and bawled like a baby, crying because my daddy didn't want me; crying for the daddy I lost with those few words; crying for the daddy I loved; crying for the daddy I wished I had. After carrying the smothered pain around for years, I finally grieved, as in death, for indeed on that day long ago I lost someone.

Irvin put his arms around me and held me.

God used this kind, loving man to draw out the hidden pain of rejection which poisoned all of my thoughts and actions. Irvin sat beside me, like a symbol of the Rock of Ages, full of acceptance and compassion, as my confession broke the pattern of negative thinking that held me bondage. Between the sobs, I forced out the words that needed to be said.

"My father said I was funny-looking when I was a little girl."

Irvin's face lit up with understanding. I continued.

"He stood far away from me and said 'she's funny-looking'…and he never held me in his arms; he never said 'I love you.' He didn't sit me on his lap, or pick me up…spend time with me… He didn't hold my hand…"

As I continued verbalizing what I had lost, I let out deep wails of sorrow, astonishing even myself. There was more to come.

"He never spent time talking to me or playing with me and didn't do anything to undo those words…so I guess I just believed that I…was…ugly and unlovable."

After a while, the torrent of tears subsided. Paradoxically, I felt a huge sense of relief. I finally recognized and admitted that Dad had hurt me. I could no longer pretend that he did not exist or matter. The heavy burden of self-deception was gone. The delusion that covered the poison that sickened my thinking was purged. Dismissing Daddy from my life did not work after all. It only masked the painful fact that I was vulnerable to his influence down to my innermost being.

Seeing this truth set me free. I was not ugly. I was only "ugly" because I *believed* I was, based on my perception of Daddy's words and actions long ago. From my adult perspective, I could clearly see now that Daddy was wrong in the way he treated me then and that I was childish in the way I reacted. My ugliness was not a fact or a truth but a childish reaction to my father's careless words and lifestyle. My spirit which was broken was now mended by the truth. I was now free—free to believe what God said about me; free to reject the lies in my head; free to accept love.

After that session on the couch with Irvin, my self-esteem began an upward spiral. I began to blossom inwardly, forgetting about myself and becoming more and more focused on others. If the first twenty-five years of my life were spent as a bird in a cage with a broken spirit, the rest would be spent keeping up with the eagles.

Chapter 19

A Wedding Takes Place

"God places the lonely in families…"
Psalm 68:6 (NLT)

I was convinced that I could spend the rest of my life with Irvin. He was heaven on earth to me. God confirmed what was in my heart. My friends approved, my church approved, my mom and Mr. Ward approved.

Without a doubt, he was my diamond in the rough. Left to myself, I would not have recognized him for in my self-destructive thinking, I was looking for a flashy kind of man with smooth tongue and a super ego. Once I let go of my delusions, God had to teach me something new—how to recognize and appreciate gold. After years of muddy thinking, it did not happen right away but it was a slow and arduous climb, but at least I was on my way.

We dated for two years, driving back and forth across the George Washington Bridge so often we felt we owned a lane or two. We even paid double toll when I drove over to see Irvin because he would always follow me back home to make sure I arrived safely. Sometimes we considered the bridge to be a big obstacle in our path. We talked of ways to avoid its traffic and tolls, wishing that we had our own little private bridge or at least very long legs that could stretch the span of the river. I think it was Irvin who brought up the fact that his uncle Erman had a canoe. I stopped complaining—I was not interested in getting that idea launched.

We spent most of our time talking in my parents' living room, going to the park or attending a church service. Every now and then, we socialized with others such as the time we went back to visit Colgate together. During the reunion, the chaplain of the university church hosted a small group of alumni, serving us snacks around a large conference-style table. As he sat at one end, he worked his way around the table with his eyes, warmly greeting each one of us personally. When his attention was focused on me and with a desire to tactfully discover the extent of my relationship with Irvin, he asked "So, Felicia, you and Walter see each other from time to time?"

"All the time soon!" I blurted, effectively killing any chance of a normal dialogue. My attempt to distract attention from myself unwittingly gave the group a good laugh, which ironically made others more relaxed. Clueless to the humor, I was simply relieved that I did not have to say another word and that it was the next person's turn.

Yet, when I was with Irvin, I talked nonstop about any and everything, craving his undivided attention. I had years of conversation bottled up inside of me. As the night hour approached ten o'clock, I talked myself to sleep as I rested my head on a pillow in his lap. He patiently listened while my speech slowly slurred to unintelligible gibberish, which upon hearing it through a dreamy fog, I startled back to wakefulness. I eventually got up and let Irvin go on home, sorry that we had to part.

As the two-year anniversary of our courtship approached, I got anxious. My biological clock was ticking away! I was over twenty-five. I knew what I wanted. I was ready to marry this man Irvin and start a family. I needed to know his intentions. It was the next topic during the series of our "couch" sessions. To my disappointment I discovered that he was definitely not anxious to get married. He offered three unspoken reasons. The first reason was fear. The second reason was understandably…fear. The third reason was, not surprisingly…fear. These emotions combined together to produce a subdued look of panic all over his face. When I pressed for an explanation he said something about the high divorce rate and not having enough money.

Well, I was downright indignant. In my mind this was nothing my God could not handle. If the Lord Jesus was big enough to find this needle-in-a-haystack marvelous man for me, I could certainly trust Him with all the details of making our marriage work. I saw absolutely no problem and felt strongly that we should marry. I was tired of waiting, tired of crossing the bridge, tired of saying goodnight as he stepped out into the cold dark night, tired of keeping my life on hold. Our future was passing by and we needed to be free to enjoy each other and raise a family before the opportunity passed. Now that I had such a fantastic friend, I was not going to let that four-letter word "fear" stop us.

One day, I simply shared *my fear* with him.

"If you don't marry me, I'll turn into a prune," I stated honestly as I sat on the couch beside him.

He nodded and smiled a bit acknowledging my comment as he wrapped an arm around me. We sat in silence for a while and he gave no more response to what I had said.

We talked about other topics. I didn't pester him. He eventually headed out the door, got in his car and drove off in the direction of the bridge. I was glad he didn't jump off.

My gentle encouragement worked. He later said my words had melted his heart. A couple of months later in May 1985 he made a special visit to my job in Harrison, NY, during our lunch hour. We went out to the nearby Stouffer's Hotel restaurant for a meal.

As we sat waiting for our food he had a coy grin on his face. I read him like a book and knew exactly what was coming.

"Give me your hand," he said as he reached under the table.

I very happily reached for his hand under the table and was thrilled when he met my expectation by awkwardly placing something cold, smooth and round on my ring finger.

I quickly withdrew my hand and was overjoyed at what I beheld. It was the most beautiful diamond ring I ever saw. I returned to my desk on a cloud, my eyes fixated on the glistening stone. I had never owned anything so valuable. I was ecstatic that he would spend hundreds of dollars at one time on me. My coworkers surrounded me with squeals of delight and congratulations.

We were married a year later in 1986, nine years after I first met him at Colgate. It was a misty, fairy-tale-like day for me. In the dressing room, which was my mom's bedroom, I was surrounded by beautiful, strong women, all of whom were my friends and supporters. There were my precious friends from King's: Tina was my maid of honor; Gaye, Debbie, and Irvin's sister, Lorraine, were bridesmaids. They looked lovely in the pale rose tea-length dresses I picked out for them. That day I remember receiving loads of well wishes and kisses, seeing many smiling faces, hearing beautiful solos, shivering in the sleeveless second-hand wedding gown I purchased from an ad in the newspaper and feeling a bit dissatisfied with my hair. But most of all, I remember my fiance's loving gaze as I walked down the aisle towards him. That image of him still warms my heart.

With our parents at our side
(left to right: Mr. and Mrs.
Johnson II; Mr and Mrs.
Cornelius Alston)

The new couple:
Mr. and Mrs. Walter Johnson, III (1986)

The wedding ceremony was over pretty quickly. It was a morning wedding beginning at ten and ending by eleven thirty. Afterwards, we took pictures in Mount Vernon's Hartley Park's gazebo. Irvin's mother's brother, Uncle Erman, a professional photographer, gave us a gift of his exquisite work in the form of our wedding album. The reception started at noon in a crowded restaurant by a marina and ended by three. Thankfully there was neither room nor time for dancing to be an issue, since it was forbidden by my church. In the absence of dance music, I tried to make the reception as jovial as I could. I ordered sparkling apple cider, provided a choice of three entrees (chicken, fish or steak), and arranged for two very comical and gifted guests to share remarks. A bridesmaids' husband and Irvin's cousin Todd, also the best man, delivered such comical remarks that they had everyone, including Irvin and me, laughing at our crazy courtship. I was pleased when I heard that these two intelligent and articulate men both went on to become successful lawyers.

Daddy showed up for the wedding! I didn't think he cared enough to come. I didn't talk about my wedding plans with him or send him an invitation. When I was deciding on who would walk me down the aisle, I told Mr. Ward that I was thinking of him since he showed more interest in me than Dad. Mother would not have that. She insisted that Dad do it, so I lost that battle.

On that day, he was there all dressed up to walk me down the aisle. At first I thought, *What nerve...he can't give me away—he never claimed me.* I don't remember if he said anything to me or brought a gift, but he was there beside me for a fleeting moment, joined in on the picture-taking afterwards and then he seemed to disappear again. According to witnesses, he was seen at the reception.

After all was over by mid-afternoon, Irvin and I drove sixty miles north to the townhouse we closed on a month earlier. Purchasing this place to live was our choice over a honeymoon. We sat down on the living room's orange/brown/gold shaggy carpet surrounded by blazing hot orange walls that reminded me of hell. Ignoring the color of intense heat around us, we proceeded to open our presents, counted the cash and made plans to fix up the house. The first priority was to repaint the orange walls soft, cool, calming shades of mint and boxwood greens and replace the carpet. We counted the gift money and it turned out to be just enough to cover the cost of the $2,000 reception.

A year after our wedding, we gained a stepfather. Mr. Ward became an official family member. He had promised me that if Irvin and I got married, he and Mom would follow right behind us. True to his word, he married Mom on August 15, 1987. For the sake of his step-grandchild growing within me, we renamed him "Papa."

Once married, I marveled at how much Daddy's interest in me increased. He began to call and visit, but I did not trust that he was genuinely concerned about me. I figured he was seeking assurance of help for the latter years, because when he visited he still spent little time with me. After dropping off his overnight bag and a uttering quick words of greetings, and maybe eating a quick meal, my adventurous dad was running off again, hanging out "who knows where" most of the day and coming back home way after the sun set. We got so few visits from our family members that Irvin and I began to look forward to Daddy's spontaneous visits.

We actually begin to make pleasant memories together when Dad was not running. We went to the local mall and posed for a Daddy-sponsored family portrait after he received money from an unknown "friend." During another visit, Irvin filmed Daddy singing "Up on the Roof" by the Drifters as I strummed the chords on the guitar. Dad could sing, and I would have loved to have heard more. These moments were rare and enriching.

Something else new occurred. Daddy started displaying affection towards me. Both the verbal and non-verbal affection made me uncomfortable since I was not accustomed to it. It was odd when he suddenly ended a dry, shallow phone conversation with an "I love you" or expected a hug and kiss on the cheek at our visits. I was content to just say hello, how are you, and greet him in person without physical contact, but he would not have it. "Give your daddy a kiss!" he'd blurt out. I wondered if he was a pervert or something. It just wasn't natural. In time, I complied even though it never felt right.

Yet, he was making an effort to be my daddy now, so a slight relationship started to form between us. He sent me a postcard after Joel was born that autumn.

> *Dear Flea, & Family*
> *Just a few lines to let you know that I am okay. To my surprise, I came to Denver, Colorado, Tuesday to do some work for the company. I hope you and family are well. I am installing communication systems and*

expansion work at the new Denver International Airport. We're working on a 300-foot-high tower. It is fantastic. Tonight we came back to the motel in a blizzard (no problems). Hope to see you soon.
Love, Dad

I didn't think much of the postcard at the time because I was in the throes of motherhood. Daddy may have been reaching out to me, but I did not feel any need to respond. It was still more comfortable keeping him at a distance.

Chapter 20

Children

"He maketh the barren woman to keep house, and to be a joyful mother of children. Praise ye the Lord."
Psalm 113:9 (King James Version)

After moving to the suburbs of Middletown, I kept my job at IBM in Westchester and, in August, Irvin found a job working for Chase Manhattan Bank in New York City. He accepted the long commute knowing that his division would move to Fort Lee, New Jersey, in November, which would considerably shorten the travel time. We both commuted over sixty miles one way each workday. There was no time for me to get acquainted with my neighbors or to feel as though I was a part of the community for I was hungry and tired by the time I got home about five thirty in the evening. I needed to prepare dinner, do the necessary chores and get ready for the next day of work.

When Irvin was home, that first summer we had wonderful times. Usually on Saturday mornings or after work if he got home early enough, we played badminton in the tiny rear yard, laughing so hard at each other's awkward movements that I was concerned our neighbors would complain about the noise we were making. At most times, we just enjoyed each other's company as he did little things to make me laugh. He played a type of "Frankenstein" by placing one stiff arm out in front of him, then swinging the other arm into place beside it and walking stiffly towards me like a zombie. I usually was laughing too much to get away.

Then there was his explanation for how fast a Concorde plane could fly. With a somber sense of intellectualism, he explained it to me.

"If your face was your face and my hand was a Concorde…"

I watched and listened carefully for the answer. He quickly swept his hand in front of my face.

"Swish," he stared at me to see if I got it.

If it is not funny on page it is because it is something that has to be seen.

Of all the ways he made me laugh in those early days, I think my favorite was his "interrogator" act. When he performed that one, I doubled over in laughter.

"What iz jour name!!!!" he demanded with a heavy foreign accent, pretending to hold a flashlight directly in my eyes.

Before I could answer the question he'd scream out.

"You lie!!! You lie!!!"

He could also make me laugh by doing really simple things like turning up one side of his upper lip and by wiggling his ears. I was very, very happy when my husband was home, which was on the weekends and holidays. Even though I did not think of his needs as I should have been (I was not interested enough in sex), he met my deep need for an attentive and loving father whenever we were together.

Though I loved being married, it was hard adjusting to my new life. As a bride in the suburbs, I was a lonely woman during the work week. Irvin arrived home from work much later than I, sometimes as late as nine if he worked overtime or traffic was bad, and on those evenings I felt very isolated from all that was familiar to me. I missed my mother's meals. I missed the convenience of walking to the places that I needed to go. I missed the friends, relatives and acquaintances that I had all around in Mt. Vernon. After commuting more than one hundred miles a day, once I was home, I did not want to get back into the car. So I remained in my all-too-quiet town home, waiting for Irvin and feeling very lonely, isolated and barren. I decided to get careless about birth control because I wanted to fill the growing emptiness. After nine months of coming home to an empty house and eating many dinners alone, I felt blessed beyond measure when I found out that I was pregnant in February 1987. The Lord removed the word "barren" from my life.

Becoming a mother took me to a new level of love—the one that involved sacrifice. First, I suffered through mornings, afternoons and evenings from a sickness that was supposed to be confined to the first part of the day. My new companions were nausea, heartburn and the toilet. Then I watched my body grow bulbously out of proportion for someone whom I never even met. By month nine, my energetic walk had turned into a slow waddle, I floated easily in the water when we relaxed at a Delaware River beach, I could not stand the smell or taste of chicken, and I was anxious to meet this little person who had put me through so many changes.

Irvin was going through his own mental adjustments to the good news. I told him the very day I found out I was pregnant that I did not want to retain the current doctor because his first concern was if I wanted to keep the baby. Irvin was proud to have been honored with the responsibility of fatherhood, but was indignant that the doctor had considered killing his child. I switched doctors to solve that problem for both of us. After the initial joy and excitement subsided, Irvin worried just a little. He questioned who this person was who was about to invade the safety and security of our home. Was he a drug pusher, or murderer or something worse? We laughed at that crazy thought and trusted God to give us someone who we could handle. He did, but our carefree way of life was over forever. Silliness was handed over to the child as we took on the role of the sober and exhausted guardians.

The first ninth months were serene compared to what came next. My labor room scene was a rated-R battle zone. The more the obstetrician told me to calm down and to get a hold of myself, the more I screamed. My body was being split apart from the hips down and he was telling me to relax. I lost all dignity as I let out the wails, kicked my legs wildly and thrashed my arms in the air. Irvin stood there watching helplessly and I could see that he was hurting along with me. He couldn't do much more than rub my back and hold my hand whenever I let him, but his presence was very comforting. When I finally pushed Joel out, I was so relieved to see him all intact that I relaxed right away as though I had been perfectly calm the entire time. I didn't even mind the afterbirth pains—I just breathed deeply through them, just as I was taught in my Lamaze classes.

The next three months were a complete fog. I operated on autopilot. I had to breast-feed Joel every two hours around the clock to keep him content. For the first time in my life, I experienced sleep deprivation and days when I never made it out of my nightgown. As Joel grew into a toddler, my constant desire was to make sure that he was happy and safe. Irvin had to wait in line.

Caring for my son was complete with hazards just like any other job. When he was seven months of age and resting in a deep sleep between his father and me, he flipped his arm in the direction of my face. His cute little fingernail went right into my right eye, stabbing the cornea. The pain was so great that I couldn't open my eye and was definitely not able to go to work that morning.

Irvin rushed me to the emergency room and I ended up wearing an eye patch for three days.

Love for my baby transformed me into his personal slave. He cried; I picked him up and rocked him. He was hungry; I fed him. He was dirty; I bathed him. He was bored; I entertained him. He was sleepy; I tucked him into his crib. His needs overshadowed mine. This was as close to agape love that I had ever journeyed. Through motherhood, I discovered sacrificial love—a steadfast, willful giving of self for the benefit of the beloved.

The Lord used this wonderful experience of motherhood to show me something about Dad. Joel looked like my father, only in infant form. As I cared for him, I could see my father as a little baby, with great potential and beauty. My heart softened towards my father. He too, like my son, had a precious beginning…a time when he did no wrong and only took in what was given to him. Were his cries answered as quickly as I responded to Joel's? Was he fed enough, burped enough, and hugged enough? He was the ninth child, born during the Depression years to a very strong, yet possibly overwhelmed mother. Over time, I learned that babies must have more than their basic physical needs met in order to thrive. If they are not given enough positive attention, loving social interactions and immediate responses to their cries on a continual basis, some aspect of their development could be stunted. Daddy's inability to be truly intimate with people may be an indication of something he experienced as a tiny, helpless being. He may have suffered through some childhood trauma that caused him to be obsessed with self-preservation, stuck in the stage that cried out, "Me, Me, Me!" Though I did not know what caused Daddy to be so distant from us, it seemed to me that his early childhood may not have been as protected as mine. I began to feel compassion for Daddy the little child, and even Daddy the adult. H needed a loving family but did not know how to obtain one. It was time to for me to allow Dad back into my life—to share with him the family that God had given me, even though it would not be comfortable.

* * *

I watched Joel grow and soon desired a playmate for him. I tried to get pregnant again when he was one year old. The first month after trying I was disappointed so I asked God for help. Again, my period came. I was devastated. I didn't have much time. I was twenty-nine years old, Joel needed his sibling to arrive soon while they could still play together and my ovaries were growing older by the minute.

One night I pleaded with God from the depths of my heart. I was in great despair because after trying for two months I was still not pregnant. I cannot imagine the anguish women go through after trying for years. As I lay there on my back, staring up into the darkness, a voice spoke quickly from that place I recognized.

"Next month, thou shalt be with child."

Then there was silence, but my head was full of questions. Lord, is that you? No answer. Was it my own mind playing tricks? No, it wasn't me. My thoughts always came out of my head, not from deep within the heart area, and I do not speak King James English. I quickly dismissed the devil. He would not give me words of hope. By process of elimination, it had to have been the Lord.

I turned towards Irvin, who was sound asleep. I woke him up and told him what I heard. He was always incredibly patient when I interrupted his sleep at night—I did not do it often. I told him about the inaudible voice that I heard in the spirit. He agreed that if it was the Lord we'd know eventually, because time would prove it. Irvin fell quickly back to sleep.

I lay awake a bit longer just thinking. Questions flooded my mind. Will my baby be a girl or another boy? What kind of gifts and abilities will my baby have? What great purpose will God call him or her to fulfill? What kind of personality will he or she have? Who will he or she look like? I tired myself out trying to figure out the future and drifted happily off to sleep.

It *was* the Lord who had spoken! He is so wonderfully good to his children. The following month I was "with child." Nine months later, we named our second son Clarence Matthew Johnson, which according to the sources I found meant "illustrious gift of God." Joel and he are twenty-one months apart. They were best buddies as children and are still best friends today.

Chapter 21

The Seven-Year Itch

"Two are better than one; …And a threefold cord is not quickly broken.
Ecclesiastes 4:9, 12 (King James Version)

Before I was married, I thought I could have it all—a full-time career, a husband, children, a house and something new in the late '80s, a commute. For a while, I juggled all of these, but soon started to drop the balls. The seventy-mile commute proved to be very difficult, so on several occasions, I requested a job transfer to a location closer to home. I was transferred to Montvale, New Jersey, which reduced the commute time to fifty minutes. By the time Joel was born, I was working at the IBM facility in Orange County, which further reduced the morning drive to thirty-five minutes. I held on to my job until 1991. That year, the popular motto of the seventies, "you can have it all," exploded into a millions pieces and floated its soot down upon me in the form of a cruel lie. I could not "have it all" without something suffering. When I realized my children were the ones being short-changed, I had to make a change.

I learned the hard way that my children needed more of my attention. When Matthew was only a toddler, he almost died. Company policy discouraged excessive absences so I did not take time off when my kids were ill with minor ailments like coughing, runny noses or sneezing. I waited until there were symptoms more serious such as fever or vomiting. Matthew developed a persistent cough one day in January, which did not ease after a few days. Other than the cough, Matthew seemed fine. Ignoring my maternal instincts, I followed the doctor's orders to give him cough syrup even though I sensed that the cough was too persistent. I did not miss a day of work that week and even went out on Saturday night to attend a friend's bridal shower in Brooklyn, leaving my mom with a supply of cough medicine and my hacking son. While at the party, Irvin and I got a call from Mom. She was concerned that Matt was not doing well. We rushed out of Brooklyn, heading at top speed back to Mt. Vernon. After about forty-five minutes of anxious travel, we rushed into Mom's house and when I saw my eighteen-month-old son, I knew right away that he was fighting for his very life. His lips were blue and his eyes wide with terror. He was not getting enough air. We rushed him to the hospital, a few blocks away, where he was given oxygen and a tranquilizer. I almost fainted watching them hook him up to monitors and tubes and fight to restrain him as they put the oxygen mask over his face. They could not do much for him there at the local hospital. He was strapped to a gurney and rushed to Westchester Medical Center. He was diagnosed with pneumonia, placed in intensive care for three days, and then prescribed asthma medication for a year. I had waited too late to take care of my son because I put my job first.

The realization that I almost lost Matthew, added to the guilt I suffered each time I left my young sons in daycare for ten hours each workday. I was determined not to neglect my children any longer. Over the next few months, I prayed fervently to the Lord. I was determined to trust Him to help me find a way to stay home with my children.

The opportunity came a few months later in 1991, when the corporation opened the severance package to secretaries, who were before that considered as critical hires. As a secretary, I was eligible and I put in my resignation. Joel was four, Matthew was two, and I was grateful that I could finally stay home and take care of my children. To supplement Irvin's income, I found part-time work in the field of education that kept me close to my sons and to home. That same year, Irvin received two raises and a bonus check on his job which made up for the loss of my income. It was no coincidence, but rather the Lord's stamp of approval on our decision.

* * *

To every situation in life, there are opportunities to err. After giving up my job and commute, I had much more leisure time than my husband so I went out alone at night to enjoy a little recreation. When Irvin was ready to go to bed on Sunday night in preparation for a long work week ahead, I went skating at a rink in New Jersey. It was an hour trip one way, but it was worth it because

I would come home feeling energized, youthful and refreshed. Sometimes Irvin went with me during a three-day weekend, but most times I went alone, addicted to the exercise, fun and sheer challenge of the sport.

During one of those late-night sessions, a young man held out his hand for me to skate with him and I accepted. In retrospect, I should have been more guarded, but it was an appealing offer. He could skate better than I and could teach me the fancy moves I desperately wanted to learn; I was already a little bored just going around in circles. Besides that, the guy smelled nice and resembled my ruggedly handsome dad. His gesture towards me made me feel accepted and it seemed like a harmless act to skate through a song or two with him. Finally, I hadn't done anything fun in a while. Irvin and I had gotten into a pattern of work and kids, stress and responsibilities and spent little time just recreating together. I didn't realize that romance had to be cultivated, so the fun in our marriage just kind of drifted away.

Our skating together was all in fun until Irvin joined me the next time. When my "coach" found out that I was married and that my husband was the man on the sideline looking at me, he understandably released my hand and avoided me for the rest of the session. I didn't appreciate that for I was determined not to be rejected by my father, pardon me, by a man again. I would be accepted and validated. Irvin's love had enabled me to grow up a bit. I was now ready to date.

I started looking for this guy to continue to teach me his moves whenever I saw him at the rink. When he sensed that I still was willing to skate with him even though I was married, he was prepared to resume his pursuit. We started talking over the phone, skating on a regular basis and sitting and chatting at the rink between songs. I tried to witness to him, but mainly I was enjoying the growing attraction we had for each other.

My feelings slowly grew out of control as I began to think too much about this guy and to anticipate talking and skating with him. I actually started resenting my husband and wished that he would step aside and allow me to date. Fleshy thoughts surfaced from a dark, depraved place within me. I found much fault with Irvin, thinking that I didn't even like him, that he was too nice, too easy-going like me, and not the kind of cool, independent guy I admired in my dad.

Irvin saw the problem, as I was acting differently towards him. He confronted me and I told him that there was someone at the rink that I skated with and talked to but that he was just a friend. I also told Irvin that I wasn't sure if I loved him. I should have added that I loved him as a father figure and that it was just the husband-wife thing that I was having trouble with. He was deeply wounded and admitted that if I wanted to be with someone else, there was nothing he could do to stop me. He prayed and put me in the Lord's hands.

As Irvin stepped aside and remained loving, steadfast and patient, like a rock, the Lord moved in and began the process of disciplining one of his wayward children.

The first smack from the rod of correction occurred in church. His Word knocked me square in the jaw while I sat on one of the blue padded stacking chairs that served as the pews. The pastor's wife preached a sermon based on Proverbs 14:1 and something atypical for me happened. I did not like the message. I listened in defiance and squirmed in my seat. That verse was describing me, *"A foolish woman tears down her home with her own hands"*(New Living Translation). Furthermore, I was irritated that my husband was sitting next to me all righteous—like he hardly did anything wrong. I was angry at myself for having adulterous thoughts and frustrated at the fact that I was in such a visible place as church—definitely not a place to be scowling. Last, I was worried. God's word was very effective in bringing to light how stupid my recent activities had been. The Lord himself had called me "foolish" and I was worried. That was the last thing I wanted to be.

Having decided that, I continued to communicate with this guy since we were skating friends and I was trying to witness to him for the Lord. The Lord continued with the discipline.

I was warned while having my own little personal devotions. More than once, I randomly opened the Bible only to find sharp-edged, convicting scriptures like Malachi 2:15, which describes one of God's purposes for marriage: *"Has not the Lord made them one? In flesh and spirit they are his. And why one? Because he was seeking godly offspring. So guard yourself in your spirit, and do not break faith with the wife (or husband) of your youth."* God was talking to me again. I got the clear impression that adultery could severely hinder the physical and spiritual fruit that come from marriage—our children and the fruit of the Holy Spirit's work in our lives as we submit to one another: love, joy, peace, patience, kindness, goodness, faithfulness, gentleness, and self-control (Galatians 5:22). I still flirted, talked and skated with him.

Then the Lord hit me where it really hurt. He used my mother. She called me up one day out of the blue and told me of a dream she had. It was of me falling in love with some guy at a roller skating rink! I was shocked! The Lord had revealed my secret to Mom, who was a Baptist! I was the one who had attended a deliverance church for three years! I was supposed to be the sanctified and holy one! This whole ordeal was becoming very humiliating! Since Mom was one of the few people I could be very candid with, I just admitted to her that she was right, but that I was not going to hurt Irvin or doing anything stupid. That satisfied her. Now I had to live up to those words.

The guy was looking less and less attractive and more and more like trouble. I was getting wary of the whole thing. I thought, *That was a good move, Lord. I'm no match for You.* The phone conversations with skating Romeo were losing their luster and the talks with my husband and true friend were increasingly satisfying. I was impressed by Irvin's faith and resiliency.

God's reproof moved to the social level. My friend Gaye, who was at my wedding and who was currently praying to have a husband of her own, had absolutely no sympathy for me. She scolded me sharply when I tried to explain my dilemma.

"You are letting Satan use you. You better repent!"

Bless her heart; she was right and as usual very honest, though I was a little taken back at the sharpness of her tone. I think the Lord was pleased.

One night when I went to bed, my conscience and the desires within me clashed so violently that I could not get to sleep. I tossed and turned as the battle of spirit against flesh waged. For the first time in my life, I wanted to throw restraint to the wind. I wanted to give in to lust, passion and wild romance.

My spirit reacted to my thoughts by putting up gigantic signs that read "STOP," "CAUTION," "WARNING," and "NO TRESPASSING." My mind rebelled and a battle commenced that kept me awake for hours.

Mind: "It would be very, very exciting and a wonderful change of pace from your boring hum-drum life right now.

Spirit: "Foolish woman, foolish woman!"

Mind: "You can finally enjoy heated, passionate sex. You won't feel like a frigid old maid. You can go. It's dark outside—no one will see you."

Spirit: "What's done in secret will be housed upon the rooftops."

Mind: "Oooo, don't listen to that! Think of the excitement!"

Spirit: "Don't tear down your own home!"

Mind: "I can call him and plan to meet him somewhere."

Spirit: "Yeah, it's a long drive and in the morning light, you'll feel like scum."

Mind: "Your marriage is so unexciting."

Spirit: "Feelings are fickle. You are attracted to fluff of no substance right now. You can work on rekindling excitement in your marriage. Remember God's word in Malachi, "do not break faith with the husband of your youth." Think of the damage this one irrational move will do. Besides, this guy really does not love you. He'll just use you and dump you. You have a faithful husband who loves you."

I was exhausted just from the fight. I decided it was easier to do things God's way and somehow fell asleep.

During the next day I looked at my children. It was clear that adultery or divorce could devastate their happy, secure lives. Just a while ago, I gave up my career to nurture my children. Was I now going to risk harming them while I sought to fulfill some strange, fleeting desire? I could too plainly foresee the consequences of divorce in my life. I trusted God to lead me to my husband and to make my marriage work. If this failed, then trusting God failed and I would be worse off than ever. I did not want my marriage to fail. I did not want to lose Irvin. I wanted to trust in God. I forced myself to pray a prayer, using a phrase I heard on the Dr. Dobson's Christian radio program, *Focus on the Family*.

"Lord, help me to *'turn my heart towards home.'* Help me to love my husband the way I should."

When I got out of line, the Lord, like the attentive father I needed, was right there to put me back on track. If I had depended on fickle emotions as a basis for my marriage, it would have unraveled right about the time of the "seven-year itch." Thankfully since the wedding day, the Lord has been the foundation of our marriage. When the pressures of life came against us, He was faithful as the third cord to hold us together.

After His correction turned me around, God showed me the wrong thinking that had led to my straying in the first place. Our marriage relationship was one-sided for too long. For years, I soaked up the love Irvin bestowed upon me like a little child, which caused my self-esteem to grow and blossom to the point where I was happy with myself and ready to give love. However, instead of directing my desire towards my husband, I continued to relate to him as a father figure and looked at another man instead. The Lord showed me that I had to start thinking of Irvin as *my husband* and reciprocating as his lover if this marriage was ever going to survive. Even though I dismissed Daddy from my life years ago, he was right there with me in marriage. His lack of love had caused me to remain the child until this painful episode forced me to grow up. I was shocked that my father's influence was so much more than I ever estimated. It is one that cannot simply be "dismissed" from one's life.

It was time to communicate to Irvin my needs as a woman. We talked about the need to spend time together, just having fun and to "date" each other in romantic settings, complete with all the frills of dressing up and looking dashing. I also needed to be more of a giver and initiator of romance, sweet-talk, compliments and things that pleased him.

It's ironic, but because of this attack on our marriage, it is stronger than ever. In a sense, it purified my love as we went through the fire. It is no longer weak and immature as it was in the beginning, based on feelings, which come and go and are up and down. It is much more secure, much deeper and solid like a rock because it is founded on God's design. We are one, intertwined and bonded together, securely moving towards the same goal, purpose and future. True intimacy is a wonderful thing. Sometimes when we sit around talking, Irvin and I laugh at the lunacy of the whole incident. It's hard for me to believe that I was tempted to wallow about in the mud, and though I laugh about it, I am still ashamed.

That following year, in July of 1994, I was pregnant again. This time, to my sheer delight, we conceived my heart's desire, a little girl. She was born the following spring and we named her Marie Lorraine, after both of her grandmothers. If I thought life was busy before, I was wrong—we were merely warming up. To juggle the load of three children, I became a stay-at-home mom, operating a daycare in my home. I made little money during those first five years of Marie's life, but I loved being there for my family, operating my own business and "turning my heart towards home." Irvin and I make sure we take time to go out skating together.

Chapter 22

The Mighty Falls

"How are the mighty fallen...!"
2 Samuel 1:25 (King James Version)

With the blessing of a daughter, two sons and a husband, the Lord had totally satisfied my deepest desire to be a part of a happy and loving family. Now, I was ready to share that with Dad. I determined to spend more time with him. In addition to visiting him during the summer months, I tried to keep in touch with him during the rest of the year by phone, but it seemed as though I had waited too late to redeem the time we lost because he was so sick during the last few years leading up to the millennium. If Dad's life had been unsteadily declining before, it greatly accelerated its downward spin after Marie was born.

From the time Dad and Mom separated, I painfully observed his life. It was like watching a horror movie from the 1960s depicting the shapeless, hideous, bulbous monster called "The Blob" slowly inch its way along, mercilessly devouring homes, possessions and people its path. Beginning in 1982, Dad began to lose everything he had of value, one by one, as if he was being stalked by this hideous creature.

In 1982, the year Mom and Dad divorced, Dad expressed a desire to remarry, but the opportunity slipped away over time. He had dinner and party dates, but no meaningful, steady relationship with any woman after Mom. I watched him lose the blessing of a good wife when he was fifty years old.

Twelve years later in 1994, he lost meaningful and steady work. He retired after working a commendable thirty years for the same company. He then desired another source of income to supplement his pension. He tried selling vitamins and copper household products. When those ventures failed, he mentioned bottling and selling the "spring water" that gushed from the end of his driveway. (Daddy liked to joke—or at least I think he was joking.) He tried preaching the Gospel, getting ordained and setting up a little church in his home, and when that idea was abandoned for whatever reason, he settled on renting out two small bedrooms in his home. There never seemed to be enough money.

The downward slide continued. Adding to the shock of dwindling income was the loss of good health, which turned out to be the hardest blow. Dad's kidneys failed about a year after he retired. At first, he did not accept this news. He sought healing and refused dialysis, but eventually succumbed to treatment three times a week. He never gave up on his search for a kidney. It remained a paramount objective. If things were not bad enough, his health was seriously jeopardized when in 1996, two years after dialysis treatments started, he was tested positive for HIV.

The look in his eyes told me something was horribly wrong when I saw him that summer. Irvin, the children and I spent a few days at a campsite in Washington, D.C. When Dad drove out to meet us, I hardly recognized him. He had lost too much weight; his face was ashen and gaunt. Wearing a wool hat in July, he drove his car around the campsite until he found us in front of our tents. After getting out of his car, he sat down on the picnic table bench, his head hunched over, his eyes wide with fear. I had never seen him like this. He didn't have much to say—there were no jokes, wisecracks about my appearance, or big plans for the future. He looked beaten. My heart ached for him, but I could do little for he never told us what was on his mind. Dad was incredibly private and independent. I always needed him much more than he needed me.

He abruptly shoved fifty dollars cash into my hand before he left. That was a lot for him to give me at any one time, and his action seemed to carry the message that money had failed him—it was no use to him anymore. I wished he had felt free enough to confide in us, but Dad fought his battles alone. We did not learn the cause of his behavior until five years later when we learned that he had been infected with HIV. His doctor asked about the source of the infection and Dad told him, "from doing a little bit of everything." Daddy had lost so much in just a few short years that it was shockingly tragic.

Over the next few years he was constantly sick, yet he continued to travel up and down the highways searching I believe for a place to call home. He spent much of his energy traveling south to the place of his childhood. In the winter of 1998, weakened by dialysis and the onset of AIDS, Daddy had tried to reestablish himself among his remaining siblings at the family home in North Carolina, but apparently he did not pay his rent and was too sick for them to care for him. I got a call to let me know that I needed to do something, but I did not pursue getting power of attorney because he was not going to cooperate with me and I did not want to fight him.

By April of 1999, he was showing signs of dementia and incompetence. In leaving his home in Maryland to travel to North Carolina, he neglected to handle his mail, set up appointments for dialysis treatments and care for himself well enough to drive the distance. During these numerous, ill-planned trips, he would become sick from toxic buildup and come close to causing accidents on the road. Even after his treatments were transferred to Burlington, he still missed appointments. Between the toxins and the weak immune system, he became very weak and confused.

One day in the fall of 1999, a cop noticed him swerving while driving and pulled him over only to discover a very sick man at the wheel. He was rushed to a local hospital. A cousin in North Carolina immediately called me to advise me to get power of attorney over him. They also told me that he had AIDS and they could not care for him there and that I needed to get control of his estate. According to my cousin, Dad had plenty of money and he carried it in a locked, black metal box in the trunk of his car that was filled with valuables.

I called Daddy to offer to help but he told me "don't call here anymore." His voice was uncaring and angry and his comment hit me hard. I felt rejected. It made me cry and I retreated back into my shell.

After speaking with a cousin, I discovered that Dad had a reason for traveling so frequently, against his own best interest, to the homestead in North Carolina. He was involved in the lawsuit against Uncle Thomas' estate. It saddened me to think that Daddy was still chasing money.

In September of 1999, we found out from Neil that Dad was admitted to a hospital in Maryland. I called and spoke to his nurse, who told me that he was in critical condition and in intensive care. He was suffering from life-threatening meningitis and was on three strong antibiotics. On September 21, I called again. A different nurse told me that Dad's fever was 105.6 during the night, but had dropped to less than 99 that morning.

I called the doctor on September 25, 1999. I got his answering service, so

I hung up. Then I dialed Neil. There was no answer. Neil suddenly had the job of trying to handle his own and Dad's affairs. He was not prepared to fight this force that continued to wreak havoc.

I called the hospital again and I spoke to a nurse. She reported that Dad was not communicating. He would open his eyes, but not obey commands and not respond verbally. A doctor came to the phone and told me the diagnosis was infection in the blood and fluid on his brain.

Irvin and I hurried to visit him. When we arrived, he was still suffering from a high fever and delirium. His legs and arms twitched uncontrollably, his eyes were wide open without seeing and he was grunting and mumbling. We could not understand a word. He had tubes in his arms and an oxygen mask over his face. The doctor spoke with us and gave us the shockingly sad news, which confirmed what his family had told us over the phone. Daddy was HIV positive. Still, there was hope. Right there in his hospital room, I played my guitar and sang hymns. Then Irvin and I prayed asking the Lord to give him a second chance at life. The doctor did not think he would survive. We left the hospital to check on his house.

Daddy and Irvin
always got along well.

Dad with his grandchildren.
Joel, Marie and Matt (left
to right (1997).

My favorite of Daddy in Korea

Daddy in the fall of 1999

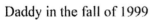

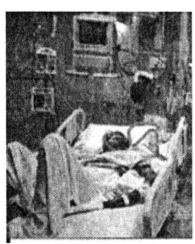

When I got to Dad's home, Neil let us in. I proceeded to search his mail and papers for information I might need. His financial standing was not the greatest for a retiree on a fixed income, with two chronic diseases. He owed over $20,000 in car and mortgage payments. I could find no life insurance policy. His assets totaled about $5,000. His annual income between social security and his pension was about $18,500. I calculated that if he sold the house and moved into a senior citizen apartment near me in Middletown, he might be able to live comfortably. I didn't consider the "little black box."

After arriving back home, I made another call to the hospital on September 28. A nurse reported, to my relief, that Dad was better. Even though she was just coming on duty, she mercifully took the time to explain Dad's condition to me. He had convulsions. He was kept on the respirator to control breathing because they felt the convulsions would interfere with breathing. He had to be heavily sedated to control anxiety and restlessness. As she spoke, I remembered my dad when he was healthy and in control. He was never still unless he was sleeping. It seemed as though he was always running, always on the go. It must have been torture for him to be confined to a bed for so long.

She couldn't answer whether or not he had been speaking. She said Dad had a pulmonary infection. She did have good news. At least his fevers had stopped. Finally, on October 5, he was moved out of ICU into a regular room. I called and spoke to a nurse who explained that Dad was hooked up to an IV, was being fed by a tube through his nose, and was restless, disoriented and confused.

On October 10, I called again to locate Dad. The responding nurse said he had been moved to a different room and she tried to connect me to his phone. I was put on hold while she got him on the phone. He sounded weak and hoarse and I could not understand his words.

Five days later, I tried again. He had been moved to a room on the east side of the hospital, but at least I spoke to an informative nurse. She said Daddy was confused. He was presently in surgery having the dialysis tube replaced in his groin area. She said that he was walking, eating and was singing Elvis Presley songs before surgery. I chuckled with relief. He was becoming himself again.

After more than three weeks in the hospital, Dad was assigned to a rehabilitation center to recover his strength. He was admitted to one in Maryland on Thursday, October 15, 1999. I called him on his birthday, October 18.

"Hi, Daddy, how are you?"

"I'm okay. Tell Neil God don't like ugly. He's trying to take my house, my money. I need ten dollars, a Coca-Cola, some chocolate. They got me way out in the country."

I thought about how different it would be today if Daddy had done more for Neil years ago. I changed the topic.

"Happy birthday!"

"Oh, is it the thirteenth?" he asked.

I didn't know if he was kidding or serious. A doctor later told me that Dad suffered dementia from the various infections. During his stay at the rehabilitation center he was caught wandering out by the highway in his hospital gown and had to be brought back several times. That was just like Dad—always going somewhere. After the stay at the rehab center, Daddy was released and I was relieved that the rehabilitation staff assigned a visiting nurse to him for a few weeks.

The Lord answered our prayer and Daddy had been given a second chance. We stopped to visit him that following summer, after attending Irvin's god sister's wedding. We did not have the children and I thought we could help out for a few hours.

It was a bright summer's day in 2000 when Irvin and I visited Dad. When I saw him, he looked shockingly ill. He had lost a lot of muscle mass and physical strength and his skin color had a grayish, unhealthy tone. It saddened me when he confessed that he did not remember our visit in his critical care unit just a few months earlier. I thought that perhaps I was making a difference by being there, and it hurt to think that my efforts in visiting him may have meant nothing at all to him. He moved about his yard unsteadily on his feet carrying a watering can around to the messy, junk-piled driveway. Suddenly the house looked much too big for him.

Unlike former times, Dad appeared solemn and uncertain during this visit. He even opened up to talk about the inevitable. He told me that he wanted me to be the executor of his estate. I was more than glad to be that for him. I appreciated the vote of confidence and looked forward to getting to know him better as he brought me up-to-date on the affairs of his estate. I had on previous occasions asked him if he had life insurance and his answer was always a very clear "yes/no." This time he told me that he was going to get the guaranteed-to-anyone life insurance advertised on television. I looked at Irvin and he looked at me. At least Dad and I were communicating.

Always comfortable in the spotlight, Dad made a little speech as Irvin captured the moment on videotape. Then he handed me his last will and testament. It basically stated his name and address and the fact that he was leaving his home, two cars, pop-up trailer and camping plot in Chincoteague, Virginia, to his three children. He added that *"my children have always been my top priority as God is my Witness."*

As the chosen executor of his will, I was not sure if I could actually do the job. I felt that Dad needed to give me more documents and records. I did not complain to him though, but accepted the position willingly, hoping that I would eventually get the tools to do the work. A hammer, some nails, access to his bank account...a forgotten insurance policy?

I looked around his house. It was dirty and in need of repair. I needed to do something to help during the few hours that we were there. I figured everyone was hungry so I looked for some food to prepare. However, before I could do that, I had to tackle organizing the kitchen. I washed dishes, bagged up the garbage, cleared off the table, and swept the floor.

When I opened the freezer section of the refrigerator, I found crystallized, uncovered food stuck together by layers of rock-hard ice and so many layers of frost that it occupied most of the freezer space. It was possible that in over several decades, Daddy never defrosted the refrigerator, so I decided to do it for him. In the process of melting the ice, I freed a dead crab, as hard as brick, from the midst of a block of ice and threw it into the trash. It seemed as though Dad had taken it right out of the ocean and tossed it into his freezer. I didn't find anything to cook, but the kitchen was cleaner.

Months of unopened mail was piled on the dining room table and stuffed in small travel bags scattered around the living room. The windows and curtains were dirty. The painted walls had faded. Soiled laundry was scattered in various places. Useless items, broken objects and junk that Dad found on the streets cluttered the floor, coffee table and chairs. A cast-iron pot-bellied stove stood in one corner with piles of paper upon it. There was an air of neglect, despair and sadness about the place that was scary and depressing.

I decided then that Daddy needed to make a change. I could see that he was no longer able to handle his house and affairs. I asked him to consider selling his home and moving into a senior citizen's home, near us in Middletown. I had it all planned in my head. He only had to cooperate. Before visiting him, I had looked into a senior housing facility, right in the heart of Middletown, situated so conveniently within walking distance of restaurants, a laundromat, the library, churches, grocery stores and barbershops. He could still be a very independent senior, but with lots of support nearby. I'd visit him regularly with the children and he would be a wonderful addition to our family gatherings (as long as he didn't make jokes about my appearance). We'd all benefit—he would have a loving family he so desperately needed, we would finally have a family member living close by, which was something we've desired over the years, and I finally would have a father because I had great hope that he would soften with age. There was only one catch to my beautiful plan. Dad would have to agree to sell his home to provide the money that we needed to establish him near us.

However, Dad was not interested in liquidating his assets. He made it clear to me that he did not want that kind of help. He suggested moving in with us and keeping his home in Maryland. I felt too defeated to tell him that we had no extra room in our cramped townhouse and would certainly need the income from the sale of his home to buy a larger house or to set him up in a senior housing, so I had no reply. The subject ended on his upbeat note.

"I'm doing okay…and the Lord is blessing me! You take care of your family. Don't worry about me. I'm in God's hands."

I didn't argue. Instead, I tried to understand his reasoning. He seemed to prefer to live by extremes, to be either totally independent or completely dependent, but neither would work. We needed a middle-ground solution here. I was also deflated by the rejection I sensed in Dad's words, which I interpreted as "stay out of my business…'cause you're not really a part of it."

Irvin and I returned to New York with very little accomplished in terms of helping Daddy. He remained in his home, as frail as he was, without long-term care after barely recovering from that close call with death last winter. I knew this was a recipe for disaster, but there was nothing I could do. All I could do was hope and pray.

I looked forward to visiting Dad the following summer of 2001, when Marie would be six years old. I wanted Daddy to see Marie again. The last time he saw her she was about two. She was developing into a beautiful little girl who looked a lot like Irvin, with butter-cream skin, a straight nose, sculptured ears and shapely lips. The shape of her face was a lot like Grandma Fields', narrow and oval. Everything about her was long and lean from her legs to her fingers.

174

She has beautiful red-brown hair. Most importantly, she had a gentle spirit, a great sense of humor and a kind, loving heart. Unlike me, I was sure she would elicit nothing but praise from her grandfather.

Now that I have received the doctor's report over the phone, I realize that the reunion between Dad and his open-hearted granddaughter was in danger of not happening. My dream of giving him warm family memories may not come true. My desire to see him prosper in some way may go unfulfilled. My big, strong daddy was fighting a foe too big for him. This enemy was not any of his three dependent, needy children. It wasn't Mom's nagging him for money. Breathing threats, hurling hard objects or disappearing from the scene were not tactics that could be used against this opponent. It was something invisible and mighty and we needed a move of God to beat it.

I kept hoping and praying for a last-minute miracle. As an adolescent in the 1970s, I regularly listened to a Christian radio station called WFME Family Radio in the evening. I heard many encouraging stories on one particular program, based in Chicago, Illinois, called *Unshackled!* This program broadcasted a series of radio dramas that portrayed real-life stories of skid-row bums, ex-convicts, drug addicts, derelicts, and other people who seemed so much worse off than Daddy. These people lost their jobs, homes, health and self-respect. Always at the end of the program there was joy as they repented and reconciled with God and their loved ones, salvaging their lives. Some conversions happened at the very last minute with the dying leaving this world victoriously looking towards eternal paradise and peacefully imparting to their bereaved a legacy of healing and redemption.

I heard other wonderful accounts, such as the story of a man who lived to be one hundred and five, as told by Jack Hayford, pastor of Church on the Way in Pasadena, California. This man lived a drunken, selfish and rebellious life for eighty-five years. As a young man, he had married a beautiful, virtuous Christian woman, who faithfully stood by him in spite of the abuse she suffered at his hand, because she was trusting in Jesus to save him. She could have divorced him, justifiably so, on the basis of his drunkenness, neglect and mistreatment. Instead, she constantly prayed for him and served him, knowing that God would honor her prayers. When she was old, she lost her eyesight. She asked her husband to read to her from the Bible each day. In light of her steadfast, unselfish devotion to him, he could not refuse. He read to her every day for three years. One day, at eighty-five years of age, as he was about to read to her, he hesitated…then fell to his knees, telling his wife that he could not *just read* anymore, but he had to now *respond*; he wanted Jesus in his life. He asked her to pray with him. He became a new person from that day on until his death twenty years later. I saw over and over again how God's Word changes people. In this particular radio broadcast, Dr. Hayford also pointed out that even Napoleon recognized the power of the Bible, exclaiming, "This is no mere book! It is a creature and it conquers everyone who opposes it!" That is true and it also lifts up anyone who honors it.

My hope now was for Dad to experience this life-changing power of God's word in a dramatic, visible way. If Daddy couldn't live, I was a least hoping for him to leave this world in the victory of reconciliation. I wanted to at least be at his side in the last moments to show that I loved him and needed some form of closure. He'll tell me his regrets, I'll tell him mine. My heart will be filled with satisfaction that we cleared things up before he breathed his last. The legacy he'd leave me would be that dad and daughter parted with healing words. I asked God again to keep him alive until we got there. I wanted this last-minute miracle. We were leaving in the morning and would be there tomorrow by early afternoon.

* * *

Early Thursday morning, around 3:00 a.m. Irvin and I were abruptly awakened to the alarming shrill of the phone ringing. Irvin scrambled quickly out of bed with arms outstretched as he stumbled to feel for the wall phone in the darkness. It was from someone at the hospital. He hung up the phone and came back to lay by my side. Then he told me. *Daddy had died…and with him all my hope of reconciliation.*

I cried. It was a deep, mournful, painful cry, full of regret and pain; full of sorrow and tragedy. I cried for the dad who I knew and for the daddy that could have been. I cried for his pains, losses and failures. I cried for all of our lost hopes, dreams, and possibilities. I cried for the worthlessness I felt and for the permanently cracked and empty pot of clay he left dangling in my hands.

Chapter 23

Season of Tears

The days of our years are threescore years and ten; and if by reason of strength they be fourscore years, yet is their strength labour and sorrow; for it is soon cut off, and we fly away. So teach us to number our days, that we may apply our hearts unto wisdom.

Psalm 90; 10, 12 (King James Version)

A seed dies and a beautiful plant takes its place. A lamb is slaughtered and it feeds a hungry family. Jesus was buried in a cave but arose full of glory three days later effectively bridging the road to eternal life for all. Even death is a part of God's plan. He uses it as a door to new life and victory. With these thoughts in mind, though I dressed that morning in a haze of grief, I had hope. Maybe Dad thought of us in death, if not in life. He may have proven his love for his children in the very end. He may have left provisions for us and through these funds I would feel his love and will be able to close up his estate, give him an honorable burial and live the remaining of my days satisfied that in the very end, Daddy affirmed his children.

The drive to the hospital was the best part of the day. There was no traffic; my mother-in-law's car performed beautifully, the weather was clear and mild and we traveled the two hundred and fifty miles in just four hours.

When Irvin and I arrived at the hospital we had no idea of where to park the car in this unfamiliar traffic-laden city. We circled around the block where the hospital was situated searching for a place to leave the car. We finally parked in an empty spot along the street, got out and walked about a block to the hospital entrance. We were directed to a waiting room where we sat for a half hour, then an hour, then an hour and a half, as I sat filled with concern over Dad's situation. My stomach rumbled from hunger but I had no appetite. After about two hours, the doctor who attended Daddy approached us. He was sensitive and patient, answering my specific questions about the last hours of my father's life. I learned that Dad had died alone, without a friend, relative or even a minister at his side. A nurse had given him some soup the day before and no, he had not asked for me. I felt despondent. Irvin comforted me, explaining that Daddy did not know that he was dying and that was why he did not call for his family.

In my ignorance, I asked to see my father's body and was instantly deterred by the hospital's rules and regulations. I could not look upon Dad's body until I had secured the services of a funeral company. I had arrived too late. If Dad had still been in a hospital bed I could have seen him, but his body had been transported to the morgue. The hospital could not bring it back out for my viewing and I could not enter the morgue to see it. We would have to hire the services of an undertaker. We were greatly disappointed. I felt a black cloud of regret and despair following me. Now that I was desperately trying to see my father I could not. Nothing was going right. Dad had not asked for me and he was snatched away before I could to see him.

We thanked the doctor for his time and left the hospital in a daze. Dad didn't have to die so quickly, I learned. He made one final and fatal mistake. In November of 2000, he admitted himself into the hospital for a kidney transplant. He didn't tell me. If only I had known of his plans, I would have called the hospital and told his doctor that he could not receive a kidney because he was HIV positive. Maybe Dad did not want anyone to interfere and therefore purposefully kept his plans private.

The surgeon did not know of his HIV status and proceeded with the operation. Dad did well for the first month and even took his immune-suppressant drugs, but by Christmas, his body was ravaged with "opportunistic infections." Now in January 2001, his lungs and brain became infested with this fast-growing fungus. I faced the very painful truth that my daddy had literally rotted to death. That information and the fact that he did not want me in the end distressed me like a blinding black cloud. I felt so overwhelmed by evil, confusion and darkness that the grieving process was much more than just grief—it was a fight against terror.

After praying for guidance, Irvin and I took the next step, which was to go directly to Dad's home to search the phone books for an undertaker. When we walked back to where we parked the car, it was nowhere in sight. The black cloud seemed to hover closer over me. I was trying to find my way about in Dad's world now, and it was frightening.

We were totally distressed. At first we thought the car was stolen, but then noticed that all of the parked cars were gone. We frantically tried to figure out what happened when we saw an obscured sign indicating that after a certain hour cars parked were towed. We breathed a quick prayer and desperately looked around for someone who could help us to retrieve our car. We spotted a hotel down the street, found the receptionist at the front desk and questioned her. She explained that they towed cars very quickly from that spot and that we could get a taxi to the traffic bureau, pay the fine and then take another taxi to the yard where the towed cars were taken. She was kind enough to call a taxi for us.

While on the way in the cab, Irvin worried that his mother's beautiful car might have been damaged or vandalized during the towing. The early darkness of winter had fallen as we exited the taxi and made our way through a dilapidated parking lot area to the traffic bureau's office. We did not know what to expect, but to our relief the attendant treated us humanely. He pitied us when we told him that we drove here from New York because my father just died at the hospital. He did not charge us the full fine of eighty dollars but we paid the thirty dollars for the towing. He then told us where we would find the car. We were very thankful and relieved that the car was undamaged and that all of our possessions, suitcases, Irvin's camcorder, and even the loose change in the coin box, were still in place.

From the hospital, it was a quick ride to Dad's home in Riverdale. Neil let us in, gave us a key to the house and then left to spend the night with some friends. Irvin and I were sullen, tired and hungry, but there was no time for food or rest. We needed to find an undertaker. Dad's home was more dismal than the last time we visited with tons of mail and papers scattered everywhere. We had to clear a space on the living room floor in order to spread out our sleeping bags and on the round dining room table to have a place to work. There was no food, heat or anything to make us feel comfortable, and it made me think of how bleak Daddy's world had become.

By the following afternoon, we were able to see Dad's body at a local funeral home we had chosen. The people at the home pulled the gurney that held his body into a small room. The lower half of his body was covered by something that looked like a giant paper towel. I looked to see if his facial expression would tell me something about his last hours. Already he had begun to deteriorate. His facial skin sagged, as he lay on his back with hands folded over his stomach. The expression on his face was one of straining, with lips tightly closed and the chin lifted up. He looked as if he was fighting to live or to be brave. My heart sank. My big, strong, independent dad seemed to have struggled to face or to stop death, totally alone, totally alienated, as though he were never connected to anyone. Dad should not have died like this. He was a father to three children who looked up to him. The way he died only emphasized the great tragedy of his life. His tragedy affected me greatly. He was a big part of my heritage, and the blob that consumed his life now loomed over mine, threatening my happiness.

After viewing Dad's body, I needed to leave and get back to my home, my life, my children, a world in which there was order. I needed a place of refuge, to regroup and to be strengthened for the battle ahead. Irvin drove most of the way back as I sat stunned at my father's crumbled world.

During the second trip we borrowed Mom Johnson's car again. This time they came up to our home to watch the children. Irvin accompanied me again as I spent the day in Dad's home, sorting through his mail and calling creditors, insurance companies, former employers and the Social Security Administration. I found answers to my questions. His scribbled will and last testament were not usable. It was not signed or notarized, and even if it was, he had nothing of value to give away. He died without life insurance. He did not own his home or the two cars in his name. Instead he owed fifty thousand dollars to two mortgage companies and ten thousand dollars on the two cars. While cleaning out his two cars before the repossession, I found the "black box." In it were some coins and his divorce papers. For some reason, he carried his divorce papers everywhere he went. This was the "treasure" he hid in the little black box.

Dad did not think of us in death. I felt the disappointment of a thousand hopes come crushing down on me. I felt worthlessness well up inside me again. I searched desperately through his things to find some proof that he loved me, that he loved us, and found nothing. He had no cash. The few thousand dollars in his banking and investments accounts a year ago had mysteriously disappeared. The five thousand dollars he received from the family lawsuit simply vanished. There were only stacks of bills with mounting debt everywhere I looked. I looked to my husband for an explanation. He very calmly reminded me of the reason why everything was gone. Though I could not see it, it was obvious to Irvin that Daddy was addicted to gambling. A few years ago, he predicted that Dad would die broke, but I did not want to believe those words. I kept hoping and believing for the best. Now Irvin repeated his observation that Daddy squandered money betting on race horses, and this time his words were extremely credible. Between Dad's serious gambling habit, his small fixed retirement income and the high costs of treating his expensive chronic diseases it was easy to comprehend how he died in debt and couldn't even think of us.

In spite of the deep pain and disappointment in my heart, I saw how I could at least show Daddy, wherever he was, that I loved him by doing something for him in the end, even though I could not do everything he asked in executing his estate. This last deed was a tiny ray of light shining through the dark cloud. During our last visit with Dad, he told me that he wanted to be buried in the plot to which he was entitled in a veteran's cemetery for his service in the Korean War. He also told me the name of the church and pastor he wanted for his funeral service. Because he shared this with me, I did purpose to do what I could to make Dad's last two wishes a reality.

While Irvin and I worked feverishly at the cluttered table in Dad's townhouse, we grew weaker from hunger by the hour. It was such a relief when a lady friend of Daddy's brought us fried chicken from a nearby fast food place. We gobbled it up realizing that except for this lone thoughtful soul, we were pretty much alone in our grief. After we ate and were revived, I called the funeral home. Without insurance, I could not afford a funeral and all that pertained to it such as embalming the body, purchasing a casket, renting a hearse and digging up a burial plot. I didn't even have the thousand dollars needed for cremation, but Irvin offered to pay for whatever kind of service I wanted and he was glad to do it. I was amazed. He had no problem with Dad as I did, but always received him without resentment. I ordered a cremation for Dad.

We finished for the day and returned to Middletown where I would prepare a simple memorial service for Daddy since there would be no funeral. After we arrived home, Irvin's parents greeted us at the door. They had stayed overnight in our home to watch the children.

Mom and Dad Johnson have always been very supportive. Mom Johnson generously sent money to us on a regular basis to help pay for Joel and Matthew's private schooling, swimming and piano lessons. Dad Johnson took the boys with him on church-sponsored historical bus tours every summer for about eight years. At holiday family gatherings, while Mom Johnson prepared delicious meals, Dad Johnson thrilled us with his literary and oratory talents, reciting beautiful poems, some of his own creation. He could recite from memory a very long poem by Paul Laurence Dunbar entitled "The Party" and when he read aloud to us Dunbar's "An Ante-Bellum Sermon" as we gathered around him one Christmas, we were amazed at his expert rendering of the early-nineteenth-century black dialect. They took our sons on vacation with them to places like Cape Cod, Massachusetts, and Atlantic City, New Jersey, and to both amateur and Broadway shows. By the time Marie was old enough to join them, they had slowed down in their travels, but they continued to impart to our family a rich and wonderful cultural experiences and tons of love and gifts. I was not surprised when at this time of my grief and sadness, they offered much assistance.

After the kids were settled in their rooms, the four of us grown-ups sat down on the living room sofa and chair to discuss our trip and my father's business. I was so overwhelmed by grief and the load suddenly dumped on me that I lost all self-control and broke down, bawling like a baby, right before my in-laws. Mom and Dad Johnson were very sympathetic. Before they left, Dad wrote out a check for five hundred dollars to help with the expenses. Their gesture of love was a big encouragement that God was with me in this sad, dark hour. It was also a big help with the cremation expenses and to Irvin it was a confirmation from the Lord that he did the right thing.

After Mom and Dad Johnson left, I knew the first thing to tackle was the memorial service. In addition to preparing the program and the obituary, I had to prepare the eulogy, which was the most challenging. By this time, I was angry and bitter and it was hard to resist the urge to complain about how Dad had failed me. Yet, I did not want to paint a false picture. Irvin cautioned me not to denounce a person who is dead at his funeral since it would serve no constructive purpose. Rather, I should focus on the person's uniqueness and purpose in life.

His advice sounded wise, so I proceeded to revise what I had written. It was a struggle. I stayed up all night long trying to get the eulogy right. I was distressed. I didn't want to make my daddy sound wonderful. I wanted to tell the truth. I wanted to talk about the person I remembered, but somehow I would have to season it with grace. I tried to go to sleep but couldn't so I got back up out of bed and spent some time praying. I went back to the computer and formatted the text for the memorial program. Using old family obituaries as guides, I created Daddy's obituary. Then I typed in the scripture I wanted read and put our son Joel down as a reader. I continued working on a decent eulogy. Finally, after many revisions, by that afternoon, I got the eulogy the way it needed to be: truthful with just a touch of humor. Irvin approved of it and that gave me confidence.

After reading it for the last time, I had to agree that Irvin was right. After taking on a softer tone, I actually laughed as I read the eulogy on February 2, 2001. What a relief to be able to laugh. In describing Daddy from a comical perspective, I was able to see his light-hearted nature as well as his uniqueness and gifts that I had never acknowledged. Dad loved to use humor, so in making his eulogy funny, I really honored him, and yet it allowed me to be honest in talking about the only dad I knew.

* * *

PERSONAL EULOGY
For Mr. Cornelius A. Alston, Sr.
(1932-2001)

Dad was there when I was little and I learned to call him Daddy. I remember his big cabinet radio and all the good music it would bring into the house. I remember him driving us to the World's Fair. Daddy loved to be on the go, and it was nice when he took us around. But, I also remember him taking us for car rides on Sunday afternoons, popping in unexpectedly on people at dinnertime. But, it was all good with Daddy! He seemed quite comfortable breaking through the barriers of social convention. Miss Manners would have worn out herself writing responses to his maneuvers.

I remember riding down to Grandmother's during the summer in his blue Rambler. I felt secure in the back seat with Dad at the wheel. He was an excellent driver and he really knew his way around. He must have driven over a million miles during his lifetime.

Daddy didn't hold me in his lap, hug me or spend time with me. I buried this pain deep inside and gave up on Daddy. I grew up hanging on to the Heavenly Father's love. I stand here well today because Jesus was with me in those early years.

Dad moved to Maryland from our home in New York when I was fifteen. I heard very little from him until I was twenty-seven and getting married. He showed up and walked me down the aisle! I thought, the nerve! Daddy had lots of nerve. He was an untamable, restless, and bold spirit, running about, searching for something for nothing. There he was, at my wedding—basking in fatherly glory—without having paid the price! He seemed to be forever on the hunt for getting some out-of-this-world bargain, for obtaining the good life, for free.

When I saw my first child, Joel, I felt God was saying, "Look, you just can't pretend your father doesn't exist… He was once a child, helpless, sweet, and innocent, like the son I have just given you." You see, my son resembled my dad, even as an infant. Every day, when I cared for my son, I got a glimpse of my dad as a child, at the beginning of his life, full of possibilities. It is easy to love a child. The ice began to melt.

I began to accept Dad in my life again as he started showing interest. In his latter years, he told me I had a nice family, and even said "I love you" more than once. Up until he got sick in 1999, he made visits each year to my home. Of course, he didn't call first. Once, we tried to get away on vacation so that he couldn't pop in on us. We only told him that we'd be somewhere in the Poconos. His ability to track us down was uncanny. We were in bed asleep; thinking there was no way he could find our exact location. Around 11:00 p.m., we were jarred from our sleep by a pounding at the door, and Daddy's unmistakable voice calling our names. We let him in quickly before he awakened everyone at the resort.

In spite of everything, I loved Dad; all three of us did. We shall miss him. I was not able to help him like I wanted to when he got ill. But I am glad that we were able to help him fulfill two desires he expressed to me concerning his death. He wanted to be buried in a veteran's cemetery, and he wanted a memorial service at his church.

I'll miss trying to tame him in his old age. I was looking forward to the challenge. My hope and wish for him now, is that he has found that "out-of-this-world" special bargain, that good life he sought without paying the price. I hope he has found it. It does exist and it was within his reach. It is in Jesus.

* * *

I think Daddy would have been pleased with the service I put together for him. The beautiful church was the one he preferred. The pastor of his choice presented the message. His favorite church musicians and soloists performed masterfully. Fellow church workers hosted a bountiful repast. A respectable number of family, friends and well-wishers attended the service, and his children said that they will miss him and wished him well, in spite of everything. I was truly glad to have been finally able to do something for my father.

After Dad's death, I learned more things about him than I learned while he was alive. I never knew that he installed the electricity in his mother's home in Burlington or spent time in Korea. A coworker presented a vivid picture of my daddy. This man got up to make remarks at the memorial service. As he spoke, he choked back tears. I was relieved to see someone else cry for Dad.

"Good morning. I'm a friend and former friend of Neil. We call him Neil instead of Cornelius. I met him somewhere in the early '60s…and uh, we were working for a company in New York called Litton Electronics and uh, over the years we moved from different places, for instance we went from Mt. Vernon up to a place called Pleasantville, and then we came back to Long Island together…then we left and came here to Maryland, same company but changes going on through life. And incidentally, I am speaking on behalf of all those people in the sixth row who worked with him, because we all know him. He was quite a guy. One thing about Neil is he was not a morning person. Early in the morning you couldn't talk to him too much [laughs and chokes up a little]. But, uh, as a human being, he was a great guy. I used to tell him sometimes, because he was very comical and very humorous, 'You know, you should be a comedian instead of working.' And uh, another thing he liked to do, he liked to play the horses once in a while, not on a big scale, but a little, you know. So he would always tell me when he won. I said, 'Neil, how come you never tell me when you lose?'

"The last time I worked with him as a one-on-one person was at the Denver Airport in Colorado. Our company was doing some work there and they needed a couple of people to go there and help out. Neil was one of the people, and I was asked to go, 'cause a lot of people didn't want to do it. So, he asked, 'Who's the other person who's going?' Once he found out that it was me, then he was quite willing to go, because…we worked together, we understood one another, we had our different opinion about things but we respected each other and we got along real well. I remember when his son was born. As a matter of fact, I have a son of his age. At times we didn't see each other for maybe a year, but one good thing about it is whenever I saw him it was like I saw him yesterday. Our friendship and relationship was always the same. The last time I saw him…he had a little place down in Virginia and he was sick and sick and so on. I cut some branches off, and some trees that were in the rear, and we spent a whole day there. I didn't see him much time after that because during that time he was telling me that he was selling his house and moving. When I called up a couple times, people said there was nobody living at this number. So I thought since maybe since he was talking about moving, maybe he sold the house and moved. And when I heard about this, I really was shocked. I knew that he wasn't feeling all best and that he was hoping that he could get this transplant. But, I tell you, anybody who knew him, or got to know him, and like I said I knew him for forty years almost, he has always been the same, a great human being, willing to help you, if he could help in anyway, he would help…I just hope that he rests in peace."

I did not know that Dad traveled to work in Pleasantville and traveled to Colorado! Once he did send me a postcard from Colorado over ten years ago, but I did not pay it much attention. I learned more about Dad in those few months after he died than I did when he was alive. I missed him sharing his experiences with me.

Neil got up and made touching impromptu remarks:

"I'm just going to say a couple of words… I miss my father. But, uh…we had a good time. We used to ride down to North Carolina. And uh, we just rode everywhere in cars. We just loved cars. We used to go to McDonald's after church. We used to go to people, our friends' houses, and uh, like Felicia said, eat…we loved cars so much; we bought about, uh, ten cars together, me and him together. We just loved the road. His road is in heaven now; he's on the heavenly cloud. I'm gonna miss my father."

Mom in her usual fashion of loving efficiency and generosity helped me tremendously after Daddy died. She and her husband, Papa Ward, paid for a van to transport my family of five, her family of four and her sister, Aunt Mary, to Maryland for the memorial service so that we could be together in one vehicle. It was very comforting to have her at my side. She covered the cost of hotel rooms for several family members and paid for several meals. Her presence at the memorial of the man who abused her revealed to me how much she loved her children.

I was very glad for any help from family and friends. Dad's sisters sent a few dollars to help bury their brother and I accepted it gratefully. My own church in Middletown sent over meals during the week between Dad's death and the memorial service, for I had no frame of mind to cook for my family.

Honoring Dad with a decent memorial service was easy compared with executing his estate. Realistically, I could not honor his wish that I settle his estate, without first pouring in at least seventy thousand dollars to save the house and cover his debts and maybe more since creditors kept crawling out of the woodwork. After studying his liabilities, I had no choice but to back out since I did not have the money. His two cars were repossessed. His furniture, clothing and personal belongings vanished into the hands of strangers. The utility companies and bank creditors sent demands for payment of for Dad's overdue accounts. Dad's house foreclosed a year later. Other bills continued to come as long as three years after his death. The invoice for his camping plot in Chincoteague was up to $6,000 three years later. The Internal Revenue Service sent me past due notices for taxes Daddy owed in 1994 and 1996, totaling over $1,300. I sent them his death certificate.

After Daddy's memorial service, my period of mourning was increasingly filled with bitterness. I became very angry with Dad for failing me in the very end. I felt cheated. I felt used. He had promised me so much and delivered nothing. I went as far as to equate him with evil. "Daddy was evil," I'd snap, as Irvin stared at me with a blank expression. That was the only word in my mind that made sense of Daddy's affairs on earth. Even though Irvin told me Dad was a gambler, I could not process with my heart how Daddy could live and die the way he did, losing everything and robbing again his children in the end unless he was evil incarnate. That evil that enveloped him peered over me like a dark, threatening vulture. Grief, fear, anger and confusion continued to weigh heavily upon me. Nothing helped me to find peace. I tried talking to a church counselor. I prayed. I talked about Dad over and over with Irvin and I was still angry and bitter. Then, I remembered that as a child I kept a journal because writing made me feel better. It provided an outlet for my emotions which I knew I needed for by this time I had learned not to simply bury pain. I began to write down the events that stood out most in my mind, hoping to find a way on paper to make sense of the craziness.

As I wrote down the story of my life as Dad's daughter, I relived good and bad memories. There were more than a few moments at the desk when I just broke down and cried. Yet in each one of those times, I saw my Savior Jesus there with me during the good times and during the hard times. Recognizing the Lord's hand in my life was a comforting balm that healed the wounds and dried the tears. As I journeyed through the years, the pattern of releasing the tears, remembering God and finding consolation was repeated over and over again. Eventually I began to heal. Eventually I forgave Daddy.

After a year of writing, I was no longer angrily storming about the house demanding that my husband admit Dad was evil. In spending many hours reflecting, I gradually moved from the seat of the victim to that of the observer. I no longer point a finger at Dad, wondering why he didn't love me the way I needed him to. Instead, I weep inside. Gone is the anger, and in its place is a solemn heaviness because I still wonder if Dad was loved enough and I saw his pain. I know we are all born into sin and into a sinful world and have to make constant choices. Dad made his choices and lived his life. I have accepted it. When I think of Dad now, I grieve for his loss and for mine.

I always wanted Dad to prosper and be well. When he left this world so disastrously, I reacted by reaching down into the fire and salvaging all that I could—my memories. They are locked away safely in this book and if this story helps someone find their way, then again the Lord has worked all things into good.

This brings me to the subject of the clay pot Dad has left with me. I will have it with me until the day I die. This shiny pot symbolizes someone so precious and marvelous to me, my big, strong daddy. It still causes sadness when I look into its emptiness. Yet, I have learned to accept and appreciate it for what it is, to recognize its strengths, and to learn from its cracks and imperfections. If all my earthly father could give me was *silver-coated clay*, the Lord has made it bearable.

I shall put my dad's clay pot up on my shelf as a remembrance that he was there, that he tried and that I loved him.

Epilogue

"The just man walketh in his integrity; his children are blessed after him."
Proverbs 20:7 (King James Version)

Today I am no longer a lonely, desolate woman, living a life void of hope
and value. Jesus has made me a new creation, a woman of great worth, full
and happy, with so much to live for.

During the very next January, one year after Daddy died, God gave us a
very special gift. Our fourth child was born, Krystal Grace, and the season of
death was turned into a season of life and new beginnings.

Krystal is the name Joel and Matt chose, and I liked it. It fit the little infant
in my arms. I was grateful for my sons' help for I was so spent from carrying
and delivering "my precious little one" that I did not have enough wits about
me to think of a first name. However, I did proclaim her middle name. It is
Grace because that's what I needed from God as I embarked on the task of
raising a child at the age when my body started to feel a bit burdensome. As
always, the Lord is faithful. He strengthens these bones and renews my
strength every day to do what I have to do. Krystal has been such a blessing
and the push we all needed to move into a larger home three years later.

I watch my husband with his children and I see beauty. Irvin is a godly father
imparting to his children gifts of great value, and they will go far in life. The
curse is broken; to God be the glory!

DOVIE
A TRIBUTE WRITTEN BY HER SON

by B. Harrison Campbell

My first recollections of my life was when I had just turned three. I was in an orphanage and my mama was crying. I didn't know why. She was just crying and I wanted her to feel better. As I grew a little older in the orphanage, I realized what it was all about. I had become three and the rules were that a child could no longer stay in the room with their mother after that. They had to be transferred to a dormitory with other children of about the same age and sex. I believe that was when my mama firmly made up her mind to leave the orphanage to seek a new husband and a new home where we could all live together again. It didn't exactly work out that way and it was a crushing blow to Mama. But that had become the norm for my mama and grandparents. They all had lived their lives from birth in dirty, dark and dangerous mining camps, going through one mine explosion that killed 30 of their friends and acquaintances. And shortly thereafter, losing several loved ones to a national and worldwide devastating disease. And traumatic deaths followed my mama and grandma throughout their lives, even my daddy, who died at the age of 40 of bee stings that left my mama with six small children, including me at the age of three weeks. But we had a Savior that led us to the greatest fraternal organizations in the world, and still the greatest ones in existence today—The Masonic Fraternity and The Order of the Eastern Star. A large part of my story deals with our lives and experiences in the Home they built for us, as well as the lives and experiences of hundreds more who came there to live with us. My mama and my grandma spent almost a lifetime in abject poverty and grief when, except for fate, they would have been among the wealthy and aristocratic families in Birmingham and Jefferson County. I have often wondered: what, exactly, went wrong?

Paperback, 142 pages
5.5" x 8.5"
ISBN 1-60672-171-2